MISTER ROBERTS

Mister Roberts

✧

A PLAY BY

THOMAS HEGGEN & JOSHUA LOGAN

WITH A FOREWORD BY JOHN MASON BROWN

RANDOM HOUSE · NEW YORK

FOR
NEDDA

FOREWORD

BY JOHN MASON BROWN

The hero who is man-sized rather than of god-like proportions; the good individual, not the fabulously noble one; the decent fellow instead of the over-virtuous prig; the person whose influence is based upon quiet example and understanding rather than upon overstatement and obnoxious moralizing, he of all heroes, though the most common in life, is the hardest to make real in either fiction or the drama. Mr. Roberts, in spite of being shadowy, was such a figure in Thomas Heggen's book. He remains such a figure, but with the shadows gone and his qualities of leadership persuasively illustrated, not described, as he is excellently played by Henry Fonda in the admirable dramatization and well-nigh perfect production which has brought *Mister Roberts* to the stage.

Every self-indulgent reader must by now have read Mr. Heggen's profoundly moving, if hilarious, sketches about life as it was endured in the Pacific aboard a drab Navy cargo vessel which never saw action. Mr. Heggen's was a remarkable book. Indeed, in my opinion it is the most valid volume about life on a ship to have been written by an American since Marcus Goodrich wrote that minor masterpiece *Delilah*.

Mister Roberts was tough-fibered, muscular, and exuberant in its animalism. Yet it was filled with compassion. Its approach to war was both wonderfully unromantic and unorthodox. It was the kind of war book that somehow just does not get written in wartime. It was a tale—more accurately, a series of tales—about young men who were the victims of frustration. Its humor, which was lusty, was born of despair. Any readers who found it funny, and only funny, missed its point entirely and established beyond dispute their own ignorance of the war.

But *Mister Roberts* was a wise book no less than an entertaining and poignant one. Its pungency may have come from the fact that its sailors did not talk as their mothers hoped they would. Its wisdom, however, came from other sources. It recognized that boredom is one of the chief conditions and horrors of war. It realized, too, that from a serviceman's point of view the Enemy was not necessarily the armed forces of Hitler or Hirohito. It was anyone over a man who could give him orders and hence serve as an impediment to his impulses.

To the company of the *AK 601* the Skipper, a cantankerous, small-minded, and smaller-souled mortal, *was* the Enemy. Every boy and man aboard the *Reluctant* hated the Captain. All of them conspired against him incessantly and ingeniously, as the ship pursued its dreary runs from Apathy to Tedium and back again, with occasional side trips to Monotony and Ennui. That Mr. Roberts shared the crew's dislike for the Captain was one reason for his popularity.

There were others. Shy youngster of twenty-six though he was, he was the buffer between what was human in the men and inhuman in the Skipper. His quiet authority made itself felt. There was something in his voice that compelled people to strain to listen. "He was the sort of leader," Mr. Heggen assured us eloquently but with the ease of a writer of fiction whose descriptions must be accepted as documented truth, "who is followed blindly because he does not look back to see if he is being followed." Roberts had gone to war to fight. He hated being inactive almost as much as he hated the Captain. After winning many battles against the Skipper, Roberts at last won for himself a transfer to combat duty. It was this transfer which cost him his life. He was on a destroyer off Japan when it was hit by a suicide plane in Mr. Heggen's concluding sketch.

All of the youth, the maleness, the pathos, and the "service" wisdom of these sketches has been captured and enhanced in *Mister Roberts* as set behind the footlights. No play about Americans at war since *What Price Glory?* has possessed the vitality and truth of this comedy of heartbreak which Mr. Heggen has fashioned from his book with Joshua Logan's brilliant aid.

Dramatizations, as a rule, prove more like sieves than containers for the virtues of a book. *Mister Roberts* is an exception. It is the gainer, not the loser, because of what has been done to it. Stymied professors of playwriting up and down the land, anxious for the sake of their students to find an answer to such an unanswerable question as how talent actually operates, could not do better than to come to their classrooms equipped with Mr. Heggen's volume and the play made from it. The differences between the two supply as illuminating instruction as can be found on the perquisites of good narrative as opposed to the needs of expert theatre.

There being no room for them on the boards, several members of the *Reluctant's* crew have been obliged to walk the plank. These characters, however, are not missed. Plenty has been offered in their place. Mr. Heggen's independent sketches have been unified, his episodes consolidated. Yet, shrewd as are the transplantings or extensions of single lines and details, the commendable simplicity of the original has not been lost.

In spite of all the canniness of its planning, the dramatization retains a superb unstudied, almost an improvised, quality. It has the art to make the difficult seem easy; the contrived, natural; the rehearsed, impromptu. Stripped to its essentials, it tells how Roberts wins a rowdy but much-needed liberty for the crew in a Pacific port and thereafter, when transferred, loses his life. Not according to the planning of classical tragedy, but in that haphazard, arbitrary, senseless way which was the tragedy, because the reality, of war. What matters, however, is the hilarity of the incidents and the seemingly anecdotal fashion in which they follow one another. What matters, too, is the energy of the speech, the originality with which boys are observed when pushed into manhood by a form of disciplined life which they despise, and the starvation or poignancy which, therefore, underlies their jokes.

The ears of playgoers and the eyes of solitary readers operating as they do on a strangely double standard of morality, the dialogue in the play is a little less dictaphonic than it was in the book. But group hearing being the ridiculous prude it is, the speech is still audacious. Colorfully and correctly so. In fact, one of the many decencies to which *Mister Roberts* can lay claim is the un-Gideonized, pro-Kinsey language its sailors talk. It is an essential part of the script's rightness. Only the prurient or the protected could object to it. The real indecency would have been to mistake Blue Jackets for blue stockings.

The *Reluctant,* as realized in Jo Mielziner's seaworthy settings, remains as unceremonious and disorderly a bucket as she was when launched in Mr. Heggen's pages. She is the kind of ship guaranteed to lay any self-respecting graduate of Annapolis low with thrombosis. She is a war casualty—the casualty of so deadly a weapon as boredom. The members of her crew continue to be as raffish, mutinous, and prankish as they ever were. But, though they may ogle hungrily through binoculars at nurses in shower rooms on shore; assemble and swig jungle juice afloat; demolish property and the Army when they land; get so roaring drunk that they have to be hauled aboard in cargo nets; and enliven their dull days at sea by fighting one another and making the Captain's life miserable, still they are a fundamentally likable lot. It is Mr. Roberts who brings out their best qualities as surely as the Captain provokes their worst.

The affection that men feel for men is one of the most devastating of emotions. It is devastating because manliness demands that it be left unphrased. Its expressions are apt to be awkward, muted, maladroit. Its very inarticulateness is part of its poignancy.

Seldom has this affection in all its innocence and trust been more movingly stated than it is in *Mister Roberts* when in the play the young sailors slink into Roberts' presence to tell him good-bye and drink his health. It is then they present him with a decoration and a citation of their own devising which he has earned because of the courage he has shown in tossing overboard the cherished potted palm the Captain has kept outside his cabin. The decoration is the "Order of the Palm"; the citation runs: "For Action Against the Enemy, Above and Beyond the Call of Duty."

At times *Mister Roberts* may come perilously close to slapstick. In its ultimate range it may be limited by its fidelity to the juvenile mind and emotions of the young men with whom it deals. But this much seems to me, at least, as self-evident as were those truths enunciated by the Founding Fathers. It is gloriously accurate in realizing its intentions. It finds supreme showmanship informed by very human values. It is superlative theatre; a miracle of production in which the script, setting, acting, and direction all fuse to create one of the most uproarious, heartwarming, and yet touching evenings Broadway has yielded in many a long year.

Mr. Logan is one of America's ablest directors. He is a master of his medium. He knows how to drain the passing moment of its full quota of tears and laughter. He is able to

FOREWORD

cast a spell over playgoers which persuades them that all clocks except those behind the footlights have, for the time being, been halted and that life itself has become the more real for having been suspended. He possesses the human touch and the magician's wand. But, creative as Mr. Logan's work has always been, it has never been more enriching than in *Mister Roberts*.

He could not have assembled a more perfect cast. Henry Fonda plays Roberts as if he had been born for it. He is to the full the unheroic hero; the shy, modest, everyday young man whose decencies and hidden strength have somehow made a leader of him. His is a quiet performance, alive with feeling, and admirable in its avoidance of sham. Its power is its understatement, its reticence, its utter and communicated honesty.

Robert Keith is no less excellent as the easygoing ship's doctor. So, for that matter, are David Wayne as the oddly inventive Ensign Pulver, and William Harrigan as the embittered, ambitious Captain whose dislike for college men is among the ruling passions of his frustrated life. As the nurse whose birthmark is not always visible, Jocelyn Brando plays, and nicely plays, the sole woman in a very male cast. When it comes, as come it must, to the brawny and obstreperous youngsters who form the *Reluctant's* crew, they all—every mother's son and Captain's terror among them—deserve a unit citation.

The Navy is brave at sea but frightened by the dictionary. It prides itself on being the silent service. Its idea of extravagant praise is a signal reading "Well Done." Fortunately, in the presence of *Mister Roberts,* playgoers do not have to be so restrained.

(From *The Saturday Review of Literature,* March 6, 1948)

MISTER ROBERTS *was first presented by Leland Hayward at the Alvin Theatre, New York City, on February 18, 1948, with the following cast:*

(IN ORDER OF APPEARANCE)

CHIEF JOHNSON	Rusty Lane
LIEUTENANT (JG) ROBERTS	Henry Fonda
DOC	Robert Keith
DOWDY	Joe Marr
THE CAPTAIN	William Harrigan
INSIGNA	Harvey Lembeck
MANNION	Ralph Meeker
LINDSTROM	Karl Lukas
STEFANOWSKI	Steven Hill
WILEY	Robert Baines
SCHLEMMER	Lee Krieger
REBER	John Campbell
ENSIGN PULVER	David Wayne
DOLAN	Casey Walters
GERHART	Fred Barton
PAYNE	James Sherwood
LIEUTENANT ANN GIRARD	Jocelyn Brando
SHORE PATROLMAN	John Jordan
MILITARY POLICEMAN	Marshall Jamison
SHORE PATROL OFFICER	Murray Hamilton

SEAMEN, FIREMEN AND OTHERS: Tiger Andrews, Joe Bernard, Ellis Eringer, Mikel Kane, Bob Keith, Jr., Walter Mullen, John (Red) Kullers, Jack Pierce, Len Smith, Jr., Sanders (Sandy) Turner

DIRECTED BY Joshua Logan

SETTINGS AND LIGHTING BY Jo Mielziner

SCENE

Aboard the U.S. Navy Cargo Ship, *AK 601,* operating
in the back areas of the Pacific

Time: A few weeks before V-E Day until a few weeks
before V-J Day

NOTE: In the U.S. Navy, all officers below the rank of Commander
are addressed as "Mister."

ACT ONE

ACT ONE

SCENE I

The curtain rises on the main set, which is the amidships section of a navy cargo ship. The section of the ship shown is the house, and the deck immediately forward of the house. Dominating center stage is a covered hatch. The house extends on an angle to the audience from downstage left to upstage right. At each side is a passageway leading to the after part of the ship. Over the passageways on each side are twenty-millimeter gun tubs; ladders lead up to each tub. In each passageway and hardly visible to the audience is a steep ladder leading up to a bridge. Downstage right is a double bitt. At the left end of the hatch cover is an opening. This is the entrance to the companionway which leads to the crew's compartment below. The lower parts of two kingposts are shown against the house. A life raft is also visible. A solid metal rail runs from stage right and disappears behind the house. Upstage center is the door to the Captain's cabin. The pilothouse with its many portholes is indicated on the bridge above. On the flying bridge are the usual nautical furnishings: a searchlight and two ventilators. Over the door is a loudspeaker. There is a porthole to the left of the door and two portholes to the right. These last two look into the Captain's cabin.

The only object which differentiates this ship from any other navy cargo ship is a small scrawny palm tree, potted in a five-gallon can, standing to the right of the Captain's cabin door.

3

On the container, painted in large white letters, is the legend: "PROP.T OF CAPTAIN, KEEP AWAY."

At rise, the lighting indicates that it is shortly after dawn. The stage is empty and there is no indication of life other than the sound of snoring from below.

CHIEF JOHNSON, a bulging man about forty, enters through passageway upstage left. He wears dungaree shirt and pants and a chief petty officer's cap. He is obviously chewing tobacco, and he starts down the hatchway, notices the palm tree, crosses to the Captain's door cautiously, peering into the porthole to see that he is not being watched, then deliberately spits into the palm tree container. He wipes his mouth smugly and shuffles over to the hatch. There he stops, takes out his watch and looks at it, then disappears down the hatchway. A shrill whistle is heard.

JOHNSON

(Offstage—in a loud singsong voice which is obviously just carrying out a ritual)

Reveille . . . Hit the deck . . . Greet the new day . . . (The whistle is heard again) Reveille . . .

INSIGNA
(Offstage)

Okay, Chief, you done your duty—now get your big fat can out of here!

(JOHNSON reappears at the head of hatchway calling back.)

JOHNSON

Just thought you'd like to know about reveille. And you're going to miss chow again.

4

STEFANOWSKI

(*Offstage*)

Thanks, Chief. Now go back to bed and stop bothering us.

(*His duty done,* JOHNSON, *still chewing, shuffles across the stage and disappears. There is a brief moment of silence, then the snoring is resumed below.*)

(*After a moment,* ROBERTS *enters from the passageway at right. He wears khaki shirt and trousers and an officer's cap. On each side of his collar he wears the silver bar indicating the rank of Lieutenant [junior grade]. He carries a rumpled piece of writing paper in his left hand, on which there is a great deal of writing and large black marks indicating that much has been scratched out. He walks slowly to the bitt, concentrating, then stands a moment looking out right. He suddenly gets an idea and goes to hatch cover, sitting and writing on the paper.* DOC *enters from the left passageway.* DOC *is between thirty-five and forty and he wears khakis and an officer's fore-and-aft cap; he wears medical insignia and the bars of Lieutenant [senior grade] on his collar. A stethoscope sticks out of his hip pocket. He is wiping the sweat off his neck with his handkerchief as he crosses above hatch cover. He stops as he sees* ROBERTS.)

DOC

That you, Doug?

ROBERTS

(*Wearily, looking up*)

Hello, Doc. What are you doing up?

DOC

I heard you were working cargo today so I thought I'd get

ready. On days when there's any work to be done I can always
count on a big turnout at sick call.

ROBERTS
(*Smiles*)

Oh, yeah.

DOC

I attract some very rare diseases on cargo days. That day
they knew you were going to load five ships I was greeted by
six more cases of beriberi—double beriberi this time. So help
me, I'm going down to the ship's library and throw that old
copy of *Moby Dick* overboard!
(*He sits on hatch cover.*)

ROBERTS

What are you giving them these days for double beriberi?

DOC

Aspirin—what else? (*He looks at* ROBERTS) Is there something wrong, Doug?

ROBERTS
(*Preoccupied*)

No.

DOC
(*Lying back on the hatch*)

We missed you when you went on watch last night. I gave
young Ensign Pulver another drink of alcohol and orange
juice and it inspired him to relate further sexual feats of his.
Some of them bordered on the supernatural!

ROBERTS

I don't doubt it. Did he tell you how he conquered a forty-
five-year-old virgin by the simple tactic of being the first man
in her life to ask her a direct question?

DOC

No. Last night he was more concerned with quantity. It seems that on a certain cold and wintry night in November, 1939—a night when most of us mortal men would have settled for a cup of cocoa—he rendered pregnant three girls in Washington, D. C., caught the 11:45 train, and an hour later performed the same service for a young lady in Baltimore.

ROBERTS
(Laughing)

Oh, my God!

DOC

I'm not sure what to do with young Pulver. I'm thinking of reporting his record to the American Medical Association.

ROBERTS

Why don't you just get him a job as a fountain in Radio City?

DOC

Don't be too hard on him, Doug. He thinks you are approximately God. . . . Say, there *is* something wrong, isn't there?

ROBERTS

I've been up all night, Doc.

DOC

What is it? What's the matter?

ROBERTS

I saw something last night when I was on watch that just about knocked me out.

DOC
(Alarmed)

What happened?

ROBERTS

(*With emotion*)

I was up on the bridge. I was just standing there looking out to sea. I couldn't bear to look at that island any more. All of a sudden I noticed something. Little black specks crawling over the horizon. I looked through the glasses and it was a formation of our ships that stretched for miles! Carriers and battleships and cans—a whole task force, Doc!

DOC

Why didn't you break me out? I've never seen a battleship!

ROBERTS

They came on and they passed within half a mile of that reef! Carriers so big they blacked out half the sky! And battle-wagons sliding along—dead quiet! I could see the men on the bridges. And this is what knocked me out, Doc. Somehow— I thought I was on those bridges—I thought I was riding west across the Pacific. I watched them until they were out of sight, Doc—and I was right there on those bridges all the time.

DOC

I know how that must have hurt, Doug.

ROBERTS

And then I looked down from our bridge and saw our Captain's palm tree! (*Points at palm tree, then bitterly*) Our trophy for superior achievement! The Admiral John J. Finchley award for delivering more toothpaste and toilet paper than any other Navy cargo ship in the safe area of the Pacific. (*Taking letter from pocket and handing it to* DOC) Read this, Doc—see how it sounds.

DOC

What is it?

ROBERTS

My application for transfer. I've been rewriting it ever since I got off watch last night.

DOC

O God, not another one!

ROBERTS

This one's different—I'm trying something new, Doc—a stronger wording. Read it carefully.

(DOC *looks for a moment skeptically, then noticing the intensity in his face decides to read the letter.*)

DOC

(*Reading*)

"From: Lieutenant (jg) Douglas Roberts
To: Bureau of Naval Personnel
16 April 1945
Subject: Change of Duty, Request for . . ."
　　(*He looks up*)
Boy, this is sheer poetry.

ROBERTS

(*Rises nervously*)

Go on, Doc.

DOC

(*Reads on*)

"For two years and four months I have served aboard this vessel as Cargo Officer. I feel that my continued service aboard can only reduce my own usefulness to the Navy and increase disharmony aboard this ship."

9

(*He looks at* ROBERTS *and rises.* ROBERTS *looks back de-fiantly.*)

ROBERTS

How about *that!*

DOC

(*Whistles softly, then continues*)
"It is therefore urgently requested that I be ordered to com-bat duty, preferably aboard a destroyer."

ROBERTS

(*Tensely, going to* DOC)
What do you say, Doc? I've got a chance, haven't I?

DOC

Listen, Doug, you've been sending in a letter every week for God knows how long . . .

ROBERTS

Not like this . . .

DOC

. . . and every week the Captain has screamed like a stuck pig, *dis*approved your letters and forwarded them that way. . . .

ROBERTS

That's just my point, Doc. He *does* forward them. They go through the chain of command all the way up to the Bu-reau . . . Just because the Captain doesn't . . .

DOC

Doug, the Captain of a Navy ship is the most absolute monarch left in this world!

10

ROBERTS

I know that.

DOC

If he endorsed your letter "approved" you'd get your orders in a minute . . .

ROBERTS

Naturally, but I . . .
(*Turns away from* DOC.)

DOC

. . . but "disapproved," you haven't got a prayer. You're stuck on this old bucket, Doug. Face it!

ROBERTS
(*Turns quickly back*)
Well, grant me this much, Doc. That one day I'll find the perfect wording and one human guy way up on top will read those words and say, "Here's a poor son-of-a-bitch screaming for help. Let's put him on a fighting ship!"

DOC
(*Quietly*)

Sure . . .

ROBERTS
(*After a moment*)
I'm not kidding myself, am I, Doc? I've got a chance, haven't I?

DOC

Yes, Doug, you've got a chance. It's about the same chance as putting your letter in a bottle and dropping it in the ocean . . .

ROBERTS

(*Snatching letter from* DOC)

But it's still a chance, goddammit! It's still a chance!

(ROBERTS *stands looking out to sea.* DOC *watches him for a moment then speaks gently:*)

DOC

I wish you hadn't seen that task force, Doug. (*Pauses*) Well, I've got to go down to my hypochondriacs.

(*He goes off slowly through passageway.*)

(ROBERTS *is still staring out as* DOWDY *enters from the hatchway. He is a hard-bitten man between thirty-five and forty and is wearing dungarees and no hat. He stands by hatchway with a cup o' coffee in his hand.*)

DOWDY

Morning, Mister Roberts.

ROBERTS

Good morning, Dowdy.

DOWDY

Jeez, it's even hotter up here than down in that messhall! (*He looks off*) Look at that cruddy island . . . smell it! It's so hot it *already* smells like a hog pen. Think we'll get out of here today, sir?

(ROBERTS *takes* DOWDY'S *cup as he speaks and drinks from it, then hands it back.*)

ROBERTS

I don't know, Dowdy. There's one LCT coming alongside for supplies . . . (*Goes to hatchway, looks down*) Are they getting up yet?

MISTER ROBERTS

DOWDY
(Also looking down hatch)

Yeah, they're starting to stumble around down there—the poor punch-drunk bastards. Mister Roberts, when are you going to the Captain again and ask him to give this crew a liberty? These guys ain't been off the ship for over a year except on duty.

ROBERTS

Dowdy, the last time I asked him was last night.

DOWDY

What'd he say?

ROBERTS

He said "No."

DOWDY

We gotta get these guys ashore! They're going Asiatic! *(Pause)* Will you see him anyhow, Mister Roberts—just once more?

ROBERTS

You know I will, Dowdy. *(Hands* DOWDY *the letter)* In the meantime, have Dolan type that up for me.
(He starts off right.)

DOWDY
(Descending hatchway)

Oh, your letter. Yes, sir!

ROBERTS
(Calling over his shoulder)

Then will you bring a couple of men back aft?
(He exits through passageway.)

DOWDY

Okay, Mister Roberts.

(*He disappears down hatchway. He is heard below*)
All right, you guys in there. Finish your coffee and get up on
deck. Stefanowski, Insigna, off your tails . . .

(*After a moment the center door opens and the* CAPTAIN
*appears wearing pajamas and bathrobe and his officer's
cap. He is carrying water in an engine-room oil can. He
waters the palm tree carefully, looks at it for a moment
tenderly and goes back into his cabin. After a moment,*
DOWDY's *voice is heard from the companionway and he
appears followed by members of the crew.*)

DOWDY

All right, let's go! Bring me those glasses, Schlemmer.
(SCHLEMMER *exits by ladder to the bridge. Other men appear
from the hatchway. They are* INSIGNA, STEFANOWSKI, MANNION,
WILEY, REBER *and* LINDSTROM—*all yawning, buttoning pants,
tucking in shirts and, in general, being comatose. The men
do not appear to like one another very much at this hour—
least of all* INSIGNA *and* MANNION) All right, I got a little
recreation for you guys. Stefanowski, you take these guys and
get this little rust patch here. (*He hands* STEFANOWSKI *an
armful of scrapers and wire brushes, indicating a spot on
the deck.* STEFANOWSKI *looks at instruments dully, then dis-
tributes them to the men standing near him.* SCHLEMMER
*returns from the bridge, carrying four pairs of binoculars
and a spy glass. He drops them next to* INSIGNA *who is
sitting on the hatch*) Insigna, I got a real special job for you.
You stay right here and clean these glasses.

INSIGNA

Ah, let me work up forward, Dowdy. I don't want to be
around this crud, Mannion.

MANNION

Yeah, Dowdy. Take Insigna with you!

DOWDY

Shut up, I'm tired of you two bellyaching! (*Nodding to others to follow him*) All right, let's go, Reber . . . Schlemmer.
(DOWDY, REBER *and* SCHLEMMER *leave through passageway right. The others sit in sodden silence.* LINDSTROM *wanders slowly over to* INSIGNA. *He picks up spy glass and examines it. He holds the large end toward him and looks into it.*)

LINDSTROM

Hey, look! I can see myself!

STEFANOWSKI

Terrifying, ain't it?
(INSIGNA *takes the spy glass from him and starts polishing it.* LINDSTROM *removes his shoe and feels inside it, then puts it back on.*)

MANNION
(*After a pause*)
Hey, what time is it in San Francisco?

INSIGNA
(*Scornfully*)

When?

MANNION

Anybody ask you? (*Turns to* WILEY) What time would it be there?

WILEY

I don't know. I guess about midnight last night.

15

STEFANOWSKI

(*Studying scraper in his hand*)

I wonder if you could get sent back to the States if you cut off a finger.

(*Nobody answers.*)

INSIGNA

(*Looking offstage*)

Hey, they got a new building on that island. Fancy—two stories . . .

(*Nobody shows any curiosity.*)

MANNION

You know, I had a girl in San Francisco wore flowers in her hair—instead of hats. Never wore a hat . . .

(*Another sodden pause.*)

INSIGNA

(*Holding spy glass*)

Hey, Stefanowski! Which end of this you look through?

STEFANOWSKI

It's optional, Sam. Depends on what size eyeball you've got.

(INSIGNA *idly looks through spy glass at something out right. Another pause.*)

INSIGNA

Hey, the Japs must've took over this island—there's a red and white flag on that new building.

MANNION

Japs! We never been within five thousand miles of a Jap! Japs! You hear that, Wiley?

16

WILEY

Yeah, smart, ain't he?

MANNION

Japs! That's a hospital flag!

INSIGNA

Anybody ask you guys? (*Nudging* LINDSTROM *and pointing to the other group*) The goldbrick twins! (*Looks through spy glass*) Hey, they got a fancy hospital . . . big windows and . . . (*Suddenly rises, gasping at what he sees.*)

STEFANOWSKI

What's the matter, Sam?

INSIGNA

Oh, my God! She's bare-assed!

STEFANOWSKI

She!

INSIGNA

Taking a shower . . . in that bathroom . . . that nurse . . . upstairs window!
      (*Instantly the others rush to hatch cover, grab binoculars and stand looking out right.*)

WILEY

She's a blonde—see!

LINDSTROM

I never seen such a beautiful girl!

MANNION

She's sure taking a long time in that shower!

17

WILEY

Yeah, honey, come on over here by the window!

INSIGNA

Don't you do it, honey! You take your time!

STEFANOWSKI

There's another one over by the washbasin—taking a shampoo.

INSIGNA

(*Indignantly*)

Yeah. But why the hell don't she take her bathrobe off! That's a stupid goddamn way to take a shampoo!

(*For a moment the men watch in silent vigilance.*)

STEFANOWSKI

Ah-hah!

WILEY

She's coming out of the shower!

MANNION

She's coming over to the window! (*A pause*) Kee-ri-mi-ny! (*For a moment the men stand transfixed, their faces radiant. They emit rapturous sighs. That is all.*)

LINDSTROM

Aw, she's turning around the other way!

MANNION

What's that red mark she's got . . . there?

INSIGNA

(*Authoritatively*)

That's a birthmark!

18

MANNION
(*Scornfully*)

Birthmark!

INSIGNA

What do you think it is, wise guy?

MANNION

Why, that's paint! She's sat in some red paint!

INSIGNA

Sat in some red paint! I'm tellin' you, that's a birthmark!

MANNION

Did you ever see a birthmark down there?

INSIGNA
(*Lowers his spy glass, turns to* MANNION)
Why, you stupid jerk! I had an uncle once had a birthmark
right down . . .

WILEY

Aww!
(INSIGNA *and* MANNION *return quickly to their glasses.*)

STEFANOWSKI
(*Groaning*)
She's put her bathrobe on!

MANNION

Hey, she's got the same color bathrobe as that stupid bag
taking the shampoo!
(*The four men notice something and exclaim in unison.*)

19

INSIGNA

Bag, hell! Look at her now with her head out of the water . . .

LINDSTROM

She's just as beautiful as the other one . . .

STEFANOWSKI

They look exactly alike with those bathrobes on. Maybe they're twins.

MANNION

That's my gal on the right—the one with the red birthmark.

INSIGNA

You stupid crud, the one with the birthmark's on the left!

MANNION

The hell she is . . .
(MANNION *and* INSIGNA *again lower their glasses.*)

INSIGNA

The hell she ain't . . .

WILEY

Awwww!
(MANNION *and* INSIGNA *quickly drop their argument and look.*)

STEFANOWSKI

They're both leaving the bathroom together. . . .
(*The men are dejected again.*)

LINDSTROM

Hey, there ain't no one in there now!

20

STEFANOWSKI
(*Lowering his glasses*)
Did you figure that out all by yourself?
(*He looks through his glasses again.*)

MANNION
(*After a pause*)
Come on, girls, let's go!

WILEY
Yeah. Who's next to take a nice zippy shower?

INSIGNA
(*After a pause*)
They must think we got nothing better to do than stand
here!

LINDSTROM
These glasses are getting heavy!

STEFANOWSKI
Yeah. We're wasting manpower. Let's take turns, okay?
(*The others agree*)
All right, Mannion, you take it first.
(MANNION *nods, crosses and sits on bitt, keeping watch
with his binoculars. The others pick up their scrapers
and wire brushes.*)

INSIGNA
(*Watching* MANNION)
I don't trust that crud.

LINDSTROM
Gee, I wish we was allowed to get over to that island. We
could get a closer look.

21

STEFANOWSKI

No, Lindstrom. They'd see us and pull the shades down.

LINDSTROM

No, they wouldn't. We could cover ourselves with leaves and make out like we was bushes—and sneak up on them— like them Japs we seen in that movie . . .

(*He starts to sneak around front of hatch, holding his wire brush before his face.* STEFANOWSKI *hears a noise from the* CAPTAIN's *cabin and quickly warns the others.*)

STEFANOWSKI

Flash Red! (*The men immediately begin working in earnest as the* CAPTAIN, *now in khaki, enters. He stands for a moment, looking at them, and then wanders over to the group scraping the rust patch to inspect their work. Then, satisfied that they are actually working, he starts toward passageway. He sees* MANNION, *sitting on the bitt, looking through his glasses and smiling. The* CAPTAIN *goes over and stands beside him, looking off in the same direction.* STEFANOWSKI *tries frantically to signal a warning to* MANNION *by beating out code with his scraper.* MANNION *suddenly sees the* CAPTAIN *and quickly lowers his glasses and pretends to clean them, alternately wiping the lenses and holding them up to his eyes to see that they are clean. The* CAPTAIN *watches him suspiciously for a moment, then he exits by the ladder to the bridge.* STEFANOWSKI *rises and looks up ladder to make certain the* CAPTAIN *has gone*) Flash White! (*He turns and looks at* MANNION) Hey, Mannion. Anyone in there yet?

MANNION

(*Watching something happily through glasses*)

No, not yet!

INSIGNA

(*Picks up spy glass and looks, and rises quickly*)
Why, you dirty, miserable cheat!
(*Instantly all the men are at the glasses.*)

LINDSTROM

There's one in there again!

STEFANOWSKI

The hell with her—she's already got her clothes on!

INSIGNA

And there she goes! (*Slowly lowers his glass, turning to* MANNION *threateningly*) Why, you lousy, cheating crud!

MANNION

(*Idly swinging his glasses*)
That ain't all. I seen three!

STEFANOWSKI

You lowdown Peeping Tom!

LINDSTROM

(*Hurt*)
Mannion, that's a real dirty trick.

INSIGNA

What's the big idea?

MANNION

Who wants to know?

INSIGNA

I want to know! And you're damn well going to tell me!

23

MANNION

You loud-mouthed little bastard! Why don't you make me?

INSIGNA

You're damn right I will. Right now!

(*He swings on* MANNION *as* LINDSTROM *steps clumsily between them.*)

LINDSTROM

Hey, fellows! Fellows!

INSIGNA

No wonder you ain't got a friend on this ship . . . except this crud, Wiley.

(*He jerks his head in direction of* WILEY *who stands behind him on hatch cover.* WILEY *takes him by shoulder and whirls him around.*)

WILEY

What'd you say?

STEFANOWSKI

(*Shoving* WILEY)

You heard him!

(MANNION *jumps on hatch cover to protect* WILEY *from* STEFANOWSKI. INSIGNA *rushes at* MANNION *and for a moment they are all in a clinch.* LINDSTROM *plows up on the hatch and breaks them apart. The men have suddenly formed into two camps—*MANNION *and* WILEY *on one side,* INSIGNA *and* STEFANOWSKI *facing them.* LINDSTROM *is just an accessory, but stands prepared to intervene if necessary.*)

MANNION

(*To* WILEY)

Look at them two! Everybody on the ship hates their guts!
The two moochingest, no-good loud-mouths on the ship!

(STEFANOWSKI *starts for* MANNION *but* INSIGNA *pulls him
back and steps menacingly toward* MANNION.)

INSIGNA

Why, you slimy, lying son-of-a-bitch!

(*Suddenly* MANNION *hits* INSIGNA, *knocking him down.
He jumps on* INSIGNA *who catches* MANNION *in the chest
with his feet and hurls him back.* WILEY *and* STEFAN-
OWSKI *start fighting with* LINDSTROM, *attempting to break
them apart.* MANNION *rushes back at* INSIGNA. INSIGNA
sidesteps MANNION'S *lunge and knocks him to the deck.*
INSIGNA *falls on him. They wrestle to their feet and stand
slugging. At this point* ROBERTS *and* DOWDY *run on from
passageway.* ROBERTS *flings* INSIGNA *and* MANNION *apart.*
DOWDY *separates the others.*)

ROBERTS

Break it up! Break it up, I tell you!

(INSIGNA *and* MANNION *rush at each other.* ROBERTS *and*
DOWDY *stop them.*)

DOWDY

Goddamn you guys, break it up!

ROBERTS

All right! What's going on?

INSIGNA

(*Pointing at* MANNION)

This son-of-a-bitch here . . .

ROBERTS

Did you hear me?

MANNION

(*To* INSIGNA)

Shut your mouth!

DOWDY

Shut up, both of you!

INSIGNA

Slimy son-of-a-bitch!
(*Picks up scraper and lunges at* MANNION *again.* ROBERTS *throws him back.*)

ROBERTS

I said to cut it out! Did you hear me? (*Wheels on* MANNION) That goes for you too! (*Includes entire group*) I'm going to give it to the first one who opens his mouth! (*The men stand subdued, breathing hard from the fight*) Now get to work! All of you! (*They begin to move sullenly off right*) Mannion, you and the rest get to work beside number two! And, Insigna, take those glasses way up to the bow and work on them! Stefanowski, keep those two apart.

STEFANOWSKI

Yes, sir.
(*The men exit.* ROBERTS *and* DOWDY *look after them.*)

DOWDY

(*Tightly*)

You seen that, Mister Roberts. Well, last night down in the compartment I stopped three of them fights—worse than that. They've got to have a liberty, Mister Roberts.

ROBERTS

They sure do. Dowdy, call a boat for me, will you? I'm going ashore.

DOWDY

What are you going to do?

ROBERTS

I just got a new angle.

DOWDY

Are you going over the Captain's head?

ROBERTS

No, I'm going around his end—I hope. Get the lead out, Dowdy.

He exits left as DOWDY *goes off right and the lights*

Fade Out

(During the darkness, voices can be heard over the squawk-box saying:)

Now hear this . . . now hear this. Sweepers, man your brooms. Clean sweep-down fore and aft. Sweep-down all ladders and all passageways. Do *not* throw trash over the fantail.

Now, all men on report will see the master-at-arms for assignment to extra duty.

Now hear this . . . now hear this. Because in violation of the Captain's orders, a man has appeared on deck without a shirt on, there will be no movies again tonight—by order of the Captain.

SCENE II

The lights dim up revealing the stateroom of PULVER *and* ROBERTS. *Two lockers are shown, one marked "Ensign F. T. Pulver," the other marked "Lt. (jg) D. A. Roberts." There is a double bunk along the bulkhead right. A desk with its end against the bulkhead left has a chair at either side. There is a porthole in the bulkhead above it. Up center, right of* PULVER's *locker is a washbasin over which is a shelf and a medicine chest. The door is up center.*

An officer is discovered with his head inside ROBERTS' *locker, throwing skivvy shirts over his shoulder as he searches for something.* DOLAN, *a young, garrulous, brash yeoman, second class, enters. He is carrying a file folder.*

DOLAN
Here's your letter, Mister Roberts. (*He goes to the desk, taking fountain pen from his pocket*) I typed it up. Just sign your old John Henry here and I'll take it in to the Captain . . . then hold your ears. (*No answer*) Mister Roberts!
(PULVER's *head appears from the locker.*)
Oh, it's only you, Mister Pulver. What are you doing in Mister Roberts' locker?

PULVER
(*Hoarsely*)
Dolan, look in there, will you? I know there's a shoe box in there, but I can't find it.
(DOLAN *looks in the locker.*)

29

DOLAN

There ain't no shoe box in there, Mister Pulver.

PULVER

They've stolen it! There's nothing they'll stop at now. They've broken right into the sanctity of a man's own locker. (*He sits in chair at desk.*)

DOLAN

(*Disinterested*)

Ain't Mister Roberts back from the island yet?

PULVER

No.

DOLAN

Well, as soon as he gets back, will you ask him to sign this baby?

PULVER

What is it?

DOLAN

What is it! It's the best damn letter Mister Roberts writ yet. It's going to blow the Old Man right through the overhead. And them big shots at the Bureau are going to drop their drawers too. This letter is liable to get him transferred.

PULVER

Yeah, lemme see it.

DOLAN

(*Handing letter to* PULVER)

Get a load of that last paragraph. Right here.

PULVER

(*Reading with apprehension*)

". . . increase disharmony aboard this ship . . ."

DOLAN

(*Interrupting gleefully*)

Won't that frost the Old Man's knockers? I can't wait to jab this baby in the Old Man's face. Mister Pulver, you know how he gets sick to his stomach when he gets extra mad at Mister Roberts—well, when I deliver this letter I'm going to take along a wastebasket! Let me know when Mister Roberts gets back.

(DOLAN *exits.* PULVER *continues reading the letter with great dismay. He hears* ROBERTS *and* DOC *talking in the passageway, offstage, and quickly goes to his bunk and hides the letter under a blanket. He goes to the locker and is replacing skivvy shirts as* ROBERTS *and* DOC *enter.*)

ROBERTS

. . . so after the fight I figured I had to do something and do it quick!

DOC

What did you do over on the island, Doug?

ROBERTS

(*Sitting in chair and searching through desk drawer*)
Hey, Frank, has Dolan been in here yet with my letter?

PULVER

(*Innocently*)

I don't know, Doug boy. I just came in here myself.

DOC

You don't know anybody on the island, do you, Doug?

ROBERTS

Yes. The Port Director—the guy who decides where to send this ship next. He confided to me that he used to drink a

31

quart of whiskey every day of his life. So this morning when I broke up that fight it came to me that he might just possibly sell his soul for a quart of Scotch.

PULVER
(*Rises*)
Doug, you didn't give that shoe box to the Port Director!

ROBERTS
I did. "Compliments of the Captain."

DOC
You've had a quart of Scotch in a shoe box?

ROBERTS
Johnny Walker! I was going to break it out the day I got off this ship—Resurrection Day!

PULVER
Oh, my God! It's really gone!
(*He sinks to the bunk.*)

DOC
Well, did the Port Director say he'd send us to a Liberty Port?

ROBERTS
Hell, no. He took the Scotch and said, "Don't bother me, Roberts. I'm busy." The rummy!

PULVER
How could you do it!

DOC
Well, where there's a rummy, there's hope. Maybe when he gets working on that Scotch he'll mellow a little.

32

PULVER

You gave that bottle to a goddamn *man!*

ROBERTS

Man! Will you name me another sex within a thousand miles . . . (PULVER, *dejected, goes up to porthole*) What the hell's eating you anyhow, Frank?

> (DOC *crosses to bunk. He sees two fancy pillows on bottom bunk, picks up one and tosses it to* ROBERTS. *He picks up the other.*)

DOC

Well, look here. Somebody seems to be expecting company!

ROBERTS

Good Lord!

DOC

> (*Reads lettering on pillowcase*)

"Toujours l'amour . . . Souvenir of San Diego . . . Oh, you kid!"

ROBERTS

> (*Reading from his pillowcase*)

"Tonight or never . . . Compliments of Allis-Chalmers, Farm Equipment . . . We plow deep while others sleep." (*He looks at* DOC, *then rises*) Doc—that new hospital over there hasn't got nurses, has it?

DOC

Nurses! It didn't have yesterday!

PULVER

> (*Turning from porthole*)

It has today!

33

DOC

But how did you find out they were there?

PULVER
(*Trying to recall*)

Now let me think . . . it just came to me all of a sudden. This morning it was so hot I was just lying on my bunk—thinking . . . There wasn't a breath of air. And then, all of a sudden, a funny thing happened. A little breeze came up and I took a big deep breath and said to myself, "Pulver boy, there's women on that island."

ROBERTS

Doc, a thing like this could make a bird dog self-conscious as hell.

PULVER
(*Warming up*)

They just flew in last night. There's eighteen of them—all brunettes except for two beautiful blondes—twin sisters! I'm working on one of those. I asked her out to the ship for lunch and she said she was kind of tired. So then I got kind of desperate and turned on the old personality—and I said, "Ain't there anything in the world that'll make you come out to the ship with me?" And she said, "Yes, there is, one thing and one thing only—" (*Crosses to* ROBERTS, *looks at him accusingly*) "A good stiff drink of Scotch!"
(*He sinks into the chair.*)

ROBERTS
(*After a pause*)

I'm sorry, Frank. I'm really sorry. Your first assignment in a year.
(*He pats* PULVER *on the shoulder.*)

34

PULVER

I figured I'd bring her in here . . . I fixed it up real cozy
. . . (*Fondling pillow on desk*) . . . and then I was going to
throw a couple of fast slugs of Scotch into her and . . . but,
hell, without the Scotch, she wouldn't . . . she just wouldn't,
that's all.

ROBERTS

(*After a pause*)

Doc, let's make some Scotch!

DOC

Huh?

ROBERTS

As naval officers we're supposed to be resourceful. Frank
here's got a great opportunity and I've let him down. Let's fix
him up!

DOC

Right! (*He goes to desk.* ROBERTS *begins removing bottles
from medicine chest*) Frank, where's the rest of that alcohol
we were drinking last night?

PULVER

(*Pulling a large vinegar bottle half filled with colorless liquid
from the wastebasket and handing it to* DOC)

Hell, that ain't even the right color.

DOC

(*Taking the bottle*)

Quiet! (*Thinks deeply*) Color . . . (*With sudden decision*)
Coca-Cola! Have you got any?

ROBERTS

I haven't seen a Coke in four months—no, by God, it's five
months!

35

PULVER

Oh, what the hell! (*He rises, crosses to bunk, reaches under mattress of top bunk and produces a bottle of Coca-Cola. The others watch him.* DOC *snatches the bottle.* PULVER *says apologetically*) I forgot I had it.

(DOC *opens the bottle and is about to pour the Coca-Cola into the vinegar bottle when he suddenly stops.*)

DOC

Oh—what shade would you like? Cutty Sark . . . Haig and Haig . . . Vat 69 . . .

PULVER

(*Interested*)

I told her Johnny Walker.

DOC

Johnny Walker it is!
(*He pours some of the Coca-Cola into the bottle.*)

ROBERTS

(*Looking at color of the mixture*)

Johnny Walker Red Label!

DOC

Red Label!

PULVER

It may look like it—but it won't taste like it!

ROBERTS

Doc, what does Scotch taste like?

36

DOC

Well, it's a little like . . . uh . . . it tastes like . . .

ROBERTS

Do you know what it's always tasted a little like to me?
Iodine.

DOC

*(Shrugs as if to say "Of course" and rises. He takes
dropper from small bottle of iodine and flicks a drop in
the bottle)*
One drop of iodine—for taste.
(Shakes the bottle and pours some in glass.)

PULVER

Lemme taste her, Doc!

DOC

(Stops him with a gesture)
No. This calls for a medical opinion.
*(Takes a ceremonial taste while the others wait for
his verdict.)*

PULVER

How about it?

DOC

We're on the right track! *(Sets glass down. Rubs hands pro-
fessionally)* Now we need a little something extra—for age!
What've you got there, Doug?

ROBERTS

(Reading labels of bottles on desk)
Bromo-Seltzer . . . Wildroot Wave Set . . . Eno Fruit
Salts . . . Kreml Hair Tonic . . .

DOC

Kreml! It has a coal-tar base! And it'll age the hell out of it! (*Pours a bit of Kreml into mixture. Shakes bottle solemnly*) One drop Kreml for age. (*Sets bottle on desk, looks at wrist watch for a fraction of a second*) That's it!

(*Pours drink into glass.* PULVER *reaches for it.* ROBERTS *pushes his arm aside and tastes it.*)

ROBERTS

By God, it does taste a little like Scotch!

(PULVER *again reaches for glass.* DOC *pushes his arm aside and takes a drink.*)

DOC

By God, it does!

(PULVER *finally gets glass and takes a quick sip.*)

PULVER

It's delicious. That dumb little blonde won't know the difference.

DOC

(*Hands the bottle to* PULVER)

Here you are, Frank. Doug and I have made the Scotch. The *nurse* is your department.

(PULVER *takes the bottle and hides it under the mattress, then replaces the pillows.*)

PULVER

(*Singing softly*)

Won't know the difference . . . won't know the difference. (DOC *starts to drink from Coca-Cola bottle as* PULVER *comes over and snatches it from his hand*) Thanks, Doc. (*Puts cap on the bottle and hides it under the mattress. Turns and faces the others*) Thanks, Doug. Jeez, you guys are wonderful to me.

ROBERTS

(*Putting bottles back in medicine chest*)
Don't mention it, Frank. I think you almost deserve it.

PULVER

You do—really? Or are you just giving me the old needle again? What do you really think of me, Doug—honestly?

ROBERTS

(*Turning slowly to face* PULVER)
Frank, I like you. No one can get around the fact that you're a hell of a likable guy.

PULVER

(*Beaming*)

Yeah—yeah . . .

ROBERTS

But . . .

PULVER

But what?

ROBERTS

But I also think you are the most hapless . . . lazy . . . disorganized . . . and, in general, the most lecherous person I've ever known in my life.

PULVER

I am not.

ROBERTS

Not what?

PULVER

I'm not disorganized—for one thing.

39

ROBERTS

Have you ever in your life finished anything you started out to do? You sleep sixteen hours a day. You pretend you want me to improve your mind and you've never even finished a book I've given you to read!

PULVER

I finished *God's Little Acre,* Doug boy!

ROBERTS

I didn't give you that! (*To* DOC) He's been reading *God's Little Acre* for over a year! (*Takes dog-eared book from* PULVER's *bunk*) He's underlined every erotic passage, and added exclamation points—and after a certain pornographic climax, he's inserted the words "well written." (*To* PULVER) You're the Laundry and Morale Officer and I doubt if you've ever seen the Laundry.

PULVER

I was down there only last week.

ROBERTS

And you're scared of the Captain.

PULVER

I'm not scared of the Captain.

ROBERTS

Then why do you hide in the passageway every time you see him coming? I doubt if he even knows you're on board. You're scared of him.

PULVER

I am not. I'm scared of myself—I'm scared of what I might do to him.

40

ROBERTS

(*Laughing*)

What you might do to him! Doc, he lies in his sack all day long and bores me silly with great moronic plots against the Captain and he's never carried out one.

PULVER

I haven't, huh.

ROBERTS

No, Frank, you haven't. What happened to your idea of plugging up the line of the Captain's sanitary system? "I'll make it overflow," you said. "I'll make a backwash that'll lift him off the throne and knock him clean across the room."

PULVER

I'm workin' on that. I thought about it for half an hour—yesterday.

ROBERTS

Half an hour! There's only one thing you've thought about for half an hour in your life! And what about those marbles that you were going to put in the Captain's overhead—so they'd roll around at night and keep him awake?

PULVER

Now you've gone too far. Now you've asked for it. (*Goes to bunk and produces small tin box from under mattress. Crosses to* ROBERTS *and shakes it in his face. Opens it*) What does that look like? Five marbles! I'm collecting marbles all the time. I've got one right here in my pocket! (*Takes marble from pocket, holds it close to* ROBERTS' *nose, then drops it in box. Closes box*) Six marbles! (*Puts box back under mattress, turns defiantly to* ROBERTS) I'm looking for marbles all day long!

ROBERTS

Frank, you asked me what I thought of you. Well, I'll tell you! The day you finish one thing you've started out to do, the day you actually put those marbles in the Captain's overhead, and then have the guts to knock on his door and say, "Captain, I put those marbles there," that's the day I'll have some respect for you—that's the day I'll look up to you as a man. Okay?

PULVER

(*Belligerently*)

Okay!

(ROBERTS *goes to the radio and turns it up. While he is listening,* DOC *and* PULVER *exchange worried looks.*)

RADIO VOICE

. . . intersecting thirty miles north of Hanover. At the same time, General George S. Patton's Third Army continues to roll unchecked into Southern Germany. The abrupt German collapse brought forth the remark from a high London official that the end of the war in Europe is only weeks away—maybe days . . .

(ROBERTS *turns off radio.*)

ROBERTS

Where the hell's Dolan with that letter! (*Starts toward the door*) I'm going to find him.

PULVER

Hey, Doug, wait! Listen! (ROBERTS *pauses at the door*) I wouldn't send in that letter if I were you!

ROBERTS

What do you mean—*that* letter!

42

PULVER

(*Hastily*)

I mean any of those letters you been writin'. What are you so nervous about anyway?

ROBERTS

Nervous!

PULVER

I mean about getting off this ship. Hell, this ain't such a bad life. Look, Doug. We're a threesome, aren't we—you and Doc and me? Share and share alike! Now look, I'm not going to keep those nurses all to myself. Soon as I get my little nursie organized today, I'm going to start working on her twin sister—for you.

ROBERTS

All right, Frank.

PULVER

And then I'm going to scare up something for you too, Doc. And in the meantime you've got a lot of work to do, Doug boy—improvin' my mind and watching my grammar. And speaking of grammar, you better watch your grammar. You're going to get in trouble, saying things like "disharmony aboard this ship!" (ROBERTS *looks at* PULVER *quickly.* PULVER *catches himself*) I mean just in case you ever said anything like "disharmony aboard this ship" . . . or . . . uh . . . "harmony aboard this ship" or . . .

ROBERTS

Where's that letter?

PULVER

I don't know, Doug boy . . . (*As* ROBERTS *steps toward him, he quickly produces the letter from the blanket*) Here it is, Doug.

43

ROBERTS

(Snatching the letter)

What's the big idea!

(ROBERTS *goes to desk, reading and preparing to sign the letter.* PULVER *follows him.*)

PULVER

I just wanted to talk to you before you signed it. You can't send it in that way—it's too strong! Don't sign that letter, Doug, please don't! They'll transfer you and you'll get your ass shot off. You're just running a race with death, isn't he, Doc? It's stupid to keep asking for it like that. The Doc says so too. Tell him what you said to me last night, Doc—about how stupid he is.

ROBERTS

(Coldly, to DOC*)*

Yes, Doc, maybe you'd like to tell me to my face.

DOC

(Belligerently)

Yes, I would. Last night I asked you why you wanted to fight this war. And you said: anyone who doesn't fight it is only half-alive. Well, I thought that over and I've decided that's just a crock, Doug—just a crock.

ROBERTS

I take it back, Doc. After seeing my task force last night I don't even feel half-alive.

DOC

You are stupid! And I can prove it! You quit medical school to get into this thing when you could be saving lives today. Why? Do you even know yourself?

44

ROBERTS

Has it ever occurred to you that the guys who fight this war might also be saving lives . . . yours and mine, for instance! Not just putting men together again, but *keeping* them together! Right now I'd rather practice that kind of medicine—Doctor!

DOC

(*Rising*)

Well, right now, that's exactly what you're doing.

ROBERTS

What, for God's sake!

DOC

Whether you like it or not, this sorry old bucket does a necessary job. And you're the guy who keeps her lumbering along. You keep this crew working cargo, and more than that—you keep them *alive*. It might just be that right here, on this bucket, you're deeper and more truly in this war than you ever would be anywhere else.

ROBERTS

Oh, Jesus, Doc. In a minute, you'll start quoting Emerson.

DOC

That is a lousy thing to say!

ROBERTS

We've got nothing to do with the war. Maybe that's why we're on this ship—because we're not good enough to fight. (*Then quietly with emotion*) Maybe there's some omniscient son-of-a-bitch who goes down the line of all the servicemen and picks out the ones to send into combat, the ones whose glands

45

secrete enough adrenalin, or whose great-great-grandfathers weren't afraid of the dark or something. The rest of us are packed off to ships like this where we can't do any harm.

DOC

What is it you want to be—a hero or something?

ROBERTS
(*Shocked*)

Hero! My God, Doc! You haven't heard a word I said! Look, Doc, the war's way out there! I'm here. I don't want to be here—I want to be out there. I'm sick and tired of being a lousy spectator. I just happen to believe in this thing. I've got to feel I'm *good* enough to be in it—to *participate!*

DOC

Good enough! Doug, you're good enough! You just don't have the opportunity. That's mostly what physical heroism is—opportunity. It's a reflex. I think seventy-five out of a hundred young males have that reflex. If you put any one of them—say, even Frank Thurlowe Pulver, here—in a B-29 over Japan, do you know what you'd have?

ROBERTS

No, by God, I don't.

DOC

You'd have Pulver, the Congressional Medal of Honor winner! You'd have Pulver, who, singlehanded, shot down twenty-three attacking Zeroes, then with his bare hands held together the severed wing struts of his plane, and with his bare feet successfully landed the mortally wounded plane on his home field. (PULVER *thinks this over*) Hell, it's a reflex. It's like the knee jerk. Strike the patella tendon of any human being and you produce the knee jerk. Look.

46

(*He illustrates on* PULVER. *There is no knee jerk. He strikes again—still no reaction.*)

PULVER

What's the matter, Doc?

DOC

Nothing. But stay out of B-29's, will you, Frank?

ROBERTS

You've made your point very vividly, Doc. But I still want to get into this thing. I've got to get into it! And I'm going to keep on sending in these letters until I do.

DOC

I know you are, Doug.

ROBERTS

(*Signs the letter. Then to* DOC)

I haven't got much time. I found that out over on the island. That task force I saw last night is on its way to start our last big push in the Pacific. And it went by me, Doc. I've got to catch it.

(*He exits.*)

PULVER

(*After a pause*)

Doc, what are you going to give Doug on his birthday?

DOC

I hadn't thought of giving him anything.

PULVER

You know what? I'm gonna show him he's got old Pulver figured out all wrong. (*Pulls small cardboard roll from under mattress*) Doc, what does that look like?

47

DOC

Just what it is—the cardboard center of a roll of toilet paper.

PULVER

I suppose it doesn't look like a firecracker.

DOC

Not a bit like a firecracker.

PULVER

(Taking a piece of string from the bunk)
I suppose that doesn't look like a fuse.

DOC

(Rising and starting off)
No, that looks like a piece of string.
(He walks slowly out of the room. PULVER goes on.)

PULVER

Well, you just wait till old Pulver gets through with it! I'm going to get me some of that black powder from the gunner's mate. No, by God, this isn't going to be any peanut firecracker—I'm going to pack this old thing full of that stuff they use to blow up bridges, that fulminate of mercury stuff. And then on the night of Doug's birthday, I'm going to throw it under the Old Man's bunk. Bam—bam—bam! *(Knocks on* ROBERTS' *locker, opens it)* Captain, it is I, Ensign Pulver. I just threw that firecracker under your goddamn bunk.
He salutes as the lights

Fade Out

(In the darkness we hear the sound of a winch and shouted orders:)

LCT OFFICER

On the AK—where do you want us?

AK VOICE

Starboard side, up for'd—alongside number two!

LCT OFFICER

Shall we use our fenders or yours?

AK VOICE

No, we'll use ours! Stand off till we finish with the barge!

Scene III

The curtain rises and the lights dim up on the deck. ROBERTS *stands on the hatch cover.* SCHLEMMER, GERHART *and another seaman are sitting on the hatch cover. They are tired and hot. A cargo net, filled with crates, is disappearing off right. Offstage we hear the shouts of men working cargo. Two officers walk across the stage. Everyone's shirt is wet with perspiration.*

ROBERTS
(*Calling through megaphone*)
Okay—take it away—that's all for the barge. On the LCT—
I'll give you a bow line.

LCT OFFICER
(*Offstage*)
Okay, Lieutenant.

ROBERTS
(*To crew*)
Get a line over!

DOWDY
(*Offstage*)
Yes, sir!

REBER
(*Off right*)
Heads up on the LCT!

ROBERTS
That's good. Make it fast.

50

(PAYNE, *wearing the belt of a messenger, enters from companionway as* DOWDY *enters from right.*)

PAYNE

Mister Roberts, the Captain says not to give this LCT any fresh fruit. He says he's going to keep what's left for his own mess.

ROBERTS

Okay, okay . . .

PAYNE

Hold your hat, Mister Roberts. I just saw Dolan go in there with your letter.

(*He grins and exits as* ROBERTS *smiles at* DOWDY.)

DOWDY

Here's the list of what the LCT guy wants.

ROBERTS

(*Reading rapidly*)

One ton dry stores . . . quarter-ton frozen food . . . one gross dungarees . . . twenty cartons toothpaste . . . two gross skivvy shirts . . . Okay, we can give him all that.

DOWDY

Can these guys take their shirts off while we're working?

ROBERTS

Dowdy, you know the Captain has a standing order . . .

DOWDY

Mister Roberts, Corcoran just passed out from the heat.

ROBERTS

(*Looks at men who wait for his decision*)
Hell, yes, take 'em off. (DOWDY *exits.* SCHLEMMER, REBER *and seaman remove shirts saying "Thanks,* MISTER ROBERTS" *and exit right.* ROBERTS *calls through megaphone*) LCT, want to swap movies? We've got a new one.

LCT
(*Offstage*)
What's that?

ROBERTS
Charlie Chan at the Opera.

LCT
(*Offstage*)
No, thanks, we've seen that three times!

ROBERTS
What you got?

LCT
(*Offstage*)
Hoot Gibson in *Riders of the Range.*

ROBERTS
Sorry I brought the subject up.

DOWDY
(*Entering from right*)
All set, Mister Roberts.

LCT
(*Offstage*)
Lieutenant, one thing I didn't put on my list because I

52

wanted to ask you—you couldn't spare us any fresh fruit, could you?

ROBERTS

You all out?

LCT

(*Offstage*)

We haven't seen any for two months.

ROBERTS

(*To* DOWDY)

Dowdy, give 'em a couple of crates of oranges.

DOWDY

Yes, sir.

ROBERTS

Compliments of the Captain.

DOWDY

Aye-aye, sir.
   (*He exits.*)

ROBERTS

(*To* LCT)

Here comes your first sling-load! (*There is the grinding sound of a winch. With hand-signals* ROBERTS *directs placing of the sling-load. Then he shouts:*) Watch that line!
   (DOWDY's *voice is heard offstage:*)

DOWDY

Slack off, you dumb bastards! Slack off!
   (PAYNE *enters.* ROBERTS *turns to him sharply.*)

ROBERTS

What!

53

PAYNE

The Captain wants to see you, Mister Roberts.

DOWDY

(*Offstage*)

Goddammit, there it goes! You've parted the line!

ROBERTS

Get a fender over! Quick! (*To* PAYNE) You go tell the Captain I'm busy!

(PAYNE *exits.* ROBERTS *calls offstage*)

Get a line over—his bow's coming in!

REBER

(*Offstage*)

Heads up!

GERHART

(*Offstage*)

Where shall we secure?

DOWDY

(*Offstage*)

Secure here!

ROBERTS

No. Take it around the bitt!

DOWDY

(*Offstage*)

Around the bitt!

ROBERTS

That's too much! Give him some slack this time! (*Watches intently*) That's good. Okay, let's give him the rest of his cargo.

54

GERHART

(*Entering quickly and pointing toward companionway*)
Flash Red!

(*He exits. The* CAPTAIN *enters, followed by* PAYNE *and* DOLAN.)

CAPTAIN

All right, Mister! Let's have this out right here and now!
What do you mean—telling me you're busy!

ROBERTS

We parted a line, Captain. You didn't want me to leave the
deck with this ship coming in on us?

CAPTAIN

You're damn right I want you to leave the deck. When I
tell you I want to see you, I mean *now,* Mister! I mean jump!
Do you understand?

(*At this point a group of men, attracted by the noise,
crowd in. They are naked to the waist. They pretend
they are working, but actually they are listening to the*
CAPTAIN's *fight with* ROBERTS.)

ROBERTS

Yes, Captain. I'll remember that next time.

CAPTAIN

You're damn right you'll remember it! Don't *ever* tell me
you're too busy to see me! Ever! (ROBERTS *doesn't answer.*
The CAPTAIN *points to the letter he is carrying*) By God, you
think you're pretty cute with this letter, don't you? You're
trying to get me in bad with the Admiral, ain't you? Ain't
you?

55

ROBERTS

No, I'm not, Captain.

CAPTAIN

Then what do you mean by writing "disharmony aboard this ship"?

ROBERTS

Because it's true, Captain.
(*The men grin at each other.*)

CAPTAIN

Any disharmony on this ship is my own doing!

ROBERTS

That's true too, Captain.

CAPTAIN

Damn right it's true. And it ain't gonna be in any letter that leaves this ship. Any criticism of this ship stays on this ship. I got a reputation with the Admiral and I ain't gonna lose it on account of a letter written by some smart-alec college officer. Now you retype that letter and leave out that disharmony crap and I'll send it in. But this is the last one, understand?

ROBERTS

Captain, every man in the Navy has the right to send in a request for transfer . . . and no one can change the wording. That's in Navy regs.

CAPTAIN
(*After a pause*)

How about that, Dolan?

DOLAN

That's what it says, sir.

56

CAPTAIN

This goddamn Navy! I never put up with crap like that in the merchant service. All right, I'll send this one in as it is—*dis*approved, like I always do. But there's one thing I don't have to do and that's send in a letter that ain't been written. And, Mister, I'm tellin' you here and now—you ain't gonna write any more. You bring one next week and you'll regret it the rest of your life. You got a job right here and, Mister, you ain't *never* going to leave this ship. Now get on with your work. (*He looks around and notices the men. He shouts*) Where are your shirts?

ROBERTS

Captain, I . . .

CAPTAIN

Shut up! *Answer me, where are your shirts?* (*They stare at him*) Get those shirts on in a goddamn quick hurry.

(*The men pick up their shirts, then pause, looking at* ROBERTS.)

ROBERTS

Captain, it was so hot working cargo, I . . .

CAPTAIN

(*Shouting louder*)

I told you to shut up! (*To the men*) I'm giving you an order: get those shirts on!

(*The men do not move.*)

ROBERTS

(*Quietly*)

I'm sorry. Put your shirts on.

(*The men put on their shirts. There is a pause while the* CAPTAIN *stares at the men. Then he speaks quietly:*)

57

CAPTAIN

Who's the Captain of this ship? By God, that's the rankest piece of insubordination I've seen. You've been getting pretty smart playing grab-ass with Roberts here . . . but now you've gone too far. I'm givin' you a little promise—I ain't never gonna forget this. And in the meantime, every one of you men who disobeyed my standing order and appeared on deck without a shirt—every one—is on report, do you hear? On report!

ROBERTS

Captain, you're not putting these men on report.

CAPTAIN

What do you mean—I'm not!

ROBERTS

I'm responsible. I gave them permission.

CAPTAIN

You disobeyed my order?

ROBERTS

Yes, sir. It was too hot working cargo in the sun. One man passed out.

CAPTAIN

I don't give a damn if fifty men passed out. I gave an order and you disobeyed it.

LCT

(*Offstage*)

Thanks a million for the oranges, Lieutenant.

CAPTAIN

(*To* ROBERTS)

Did you give that LCT fresh fruit?

58

ROBERTS

Yes, sir. We've got plenty, Captain. They've been out for two months.

CAPTAIN

I've taken all the crap from you that I'm going to. You've just got yourself ten days in your room. Ten days, Mister! Ten days!

ROBERTS

Very well, Captain. Do you relieve me here?

CAPTAIN

You're damn right, I relieve you. You can go to your room for ten days! See how you like that!

LCT

(*Offstage*)

We're waiting on you, Lieutenant. We gotta shove off.
(ROBERTS *gives the megaphone to the* CAPTAIN *and starts off. The* CAPTAIN *looks in direction of the* LCT *then calls to* ROBERTS.)

CAPTAIN

Where do you think you're going?

ROBERTS

(*Pretending surprise*)

To my room, Captain!

CAPTAIN

Get back to that cargo! I'll let you know when you have ten days in your room and you'll damn well know it! You're going to stay right here and do your job! (ROBERTS *crosses to the crew. The* CAPTAIN *slams the megaphone into* ROBERTS' *stomach.* PULVER *enters around the corner of the house, sees the* CAPTAIN *and starts to go back. The* CAPTAIN *sees* PULVER *and shouts:*) Who's that? Who's that officer there?

PULVER
(*Turning*)

Me, sir?

CAPTAIN

Yes, you. Come here, boy. (PULVER *approaches in great confusion and can think of nothing better to do than salute. This visibly startles the* CAPTAIN) Why, you're one of my officers!

PULVER

Yes, sir.

CAPTAIN

What s your name again?

PULVER

Ensign Pulver, sir.
(*He salutes again. The* CAPTAIN, *amazed, returns the salute, then says for the benefit of* ROBERTS *and the crew:*)

CAPTAIN

By God, I'm glad to see one on this ship knows how to salute. (*Then to* PULVER) Pulver . . . oh, yes . . . Pulver. How is it I never see you around?

PULVER
(*Terrified*)
I've wondered about that myself, sir.

CAPTAIN

What's your job?

60

PULVER

(*Trembling*)

Officer in charge of laundry and morale, sir.

CAPTAIN

How long you been aboard?

PULVER

Fourteen months, sir.

CAPTAIN

Fourteen months! You spend most of your time down in the laundry, eh?

PULVER

Most of the time, sir. Yes, sir.

(ROBERTS *turns his face to hide his laughter.*)

CAPTAIN

Well, you do a good job, Pulver, and . . . you know I'd like to see more of you. Why don't you have lunch with me in my cabin today?

PULVER

Oh, I can't today.

CAPTAIN

Can't? Why not?

PULVER

I'm on my way over to the hospital on the island. I've got to go pick up a piece . . . of medical equipment.

ROBERTS

(*Calling over*)

Why, I'll take care of that, Frank.

61

CAPTAIN

That's right, Roberts. You finish here and you go over and fetch it.

ROBERTS

Yes, sir.
> (*He nods and turns away grinning.*)

CAPTAIN
> (*To* PULVER)

Well, how about it?

PULVER

This is something I've got to take care of myself, sir. If you don't mind, sir.

CAPTAIN

Well, some other time then.

PULVER

Yes, sir. Thank you, sir.

CAPTAIN

Okay, Pulver.
> (*The* CAPTAIN *baits another salute from* PULVER, *then exits.* PULVER *watches him go, then starts to sneak off.*)

ROBERTS
> (*Grinning and mimicking the* CAPTAIN)

Oh, boy! (PULVER *stops uneasily.* ROBERTS *salutes him*) I want to see more of you, Pulver!

PULVER
> (*Furiously*)

That son-of-a-bitch! Pretending he doesn't know me!
> (*He looks at watch and exits.* ROBERTS *turns laughing to the crew who are standing rather solemnly.*)

DOWDY

(*Quietly*)

Nice going, Mister Roberts.

SCHLEMMER

It was really beautiful the way you read the Old Man off!

GERHART

Are you going to send in that letter next week, Mister Roberts?

ROBERTS

Are we, Dolan?

DOLAN

You're damn right we are! And I'm the baby who's going to deliver it!

SCHLEMMER

He said he'd fix you good. What do you think he'll do?

REBER

You got a promotion coming up, haven't you?

SCHLEMMER

Yeah. Could he stop that or something?

DOLAN

Promotion! This is Mister Roberts. You think he gives a good hoot-in-hell about another lousy stripe?

ALL

Yeah.

GERHART

Hey, Mister Roberts, can I take the letter in next week?

63

DOLAN

(*Indignantly*)

You can like hell! That's my job—isn't it, Mister Roberts?

GERHART

Can I, Mister Roberts?

ROBERTS

I'm afraid I've promised that job to Dolan.

DOLAN

(*Pushing* GERHART *away*)

You heard him. (*To* ROBERTS) We gotta write a really hot one next week.

ROBERTS

Got any asbestos paper?

He starts off, the men follow happily as the lights

Fade Out

Scene IV

The lights come up immediately on the main set. REBER *and* GERHART *enter from right passageway. As they get around the corner of the house, they break into a run.* REBER *dashes off through left passageway.*

GERHART

(Excitedly, descending hatchway)

Hey, Schlemmer! Schlemmer!

(MISS GIRARD, *a young, attractive, blonde Army nurse, and* PULVER *enter from right passageway.*)

PULVER

Well, here it is.

MISS GIRARD

This is a ship?

PULVER

Unh-hunh.

MISS GIRARD

My sister and I flew over some warships on our way out from the States and they looked so busy—men running around like mad.

PULVER

It's kinda busy sometimes up on deck.

MISS GIRARD

Oh, you mean you've seen a lot of action?

PULVER

Well, I sure as hell haven't had much in the last year . . .
Oh, battle action! Yeah . . . Yeah . . .

MISS GIRARD

Then you must have a lot of B.F. on here.

PULVER

Hunh?

MISS GIRARD

You know—battle fatigue?

PULVER

Yeah, we have a lot of that.

MISS GIRARD

Isn't that too bad! But they briefed us to expect a lot of
that out here. (*Pause*) Say, you haven't felt any yourself, have
you?

PULVER

I guess I had a little touch of it . . . just a scratch.

MISS GIRARD

You know what you should do then? You should sleep
more.

PULVER

Yeah.

MISS GIRARD

What's your job on the ship?

PULVER

Me? I'm . . . Executive Officer . . .

MISS GIRARD

But I thought that Executive Officers had to be at least a . . .

PULVER

Say, you know what I was thinking? That we should have that little old drink of Scotcharoo right now—

MISS GIRARD

I think so too. You know, I just love Scotch. I've just learned to drink it since I've joined the Army. But I'm already an absolute connoisseur.

PULVER

(*Dismayed*)

Oh, you are?

MISS GIRARD

My twin sister has a nickname for me that's partly because I like a particular brand of Scotch . . . (*Giggles*) and partly because of a little personal thing about me that you wouldn't understand. Do you know what she calls me? "Red Label!" (*They both laugh*) What are you laughing at? You don't know what I'm talking about—and what's more you never will.

PULVER

What I was laughing about is—that's the kind I've got.

MISS GIRARD

Red Label! Oh, you're God's gift to a thirsty nurstie! But where can we drink it? This is a Navy ship . . . isn't it?

PULVER

Oh, yeah, yeah, we'll have to be careful . . . We mustn't be seen . . . Lemme see, where shall we go . . . (*Considers*) I have it! We'll go back to my cabin. Nobody'd bother us there.

MISS GIRARD

Oh, you're what our outfit calls an operator. But you look harmless to me.

PULVER

Oh, I don't know about that.

MISS GIRARD

What's your first name—Harmless?

PULVER

Frank.

MISS GIRARD

Hello, Frank. Mine's Ann.

PULVER

Hello, Ann.

MISS GIRARD

All right. We'll have one nice little sip in your room.

PULVER

Right this way.

(*They start off toward left passageway.* INSIGNA, MANNION, STEFANOWSKI, WILEY *and* LINDSTROM *enter from right, carrying the spy glass and binoculars.* STEFANOWSKI *trips on hatch cover.* MISS GIRARD *and* PULVER *turn*)

Hello, Mannion . . . Insigna . . . Stefanowski . . .

MANNION

(*Hoarsely*)

Hello, Mister Pulver . . .

PULVER

This is—Lieutenant Girard.

(*The men murmur a greeting.*)

MISS GIRARD

What're you all doing with those glasses?

INSIGNA

We're . . . cleaning them.

(*Suddenly pulls out shirt tail and begins lamely polishing spy glass. The others follow his example. More men crowd onto the stage.*)

PULVER

Well, don't work too hard . . . (*They turn to leave, but find themselves hemmed in by the men*) It's getting a little stuffy up here, I guess we better . . .

(ROBERTS *enters, very excited, carrying a piece of paper and a small book.*)

ROBERTS

(*Entering*)

Hey, Insigna . . . Mannion . . . get a load of this . . . Hey, Frank . . . (*He stops short seeing* MISS GIRARD.)

PULVER

Hiya, Doug boy! This is Ann Girard—Doug Roberts.

ROBERTS

How do you do?

MISS GIRARD

(*Beaming*)

How do you do? You're Frank's roommate. He's told me all about you.

ROBERTS

Really?

MISS GIRARD

What are you doing on this ship?

ROBERTS

Now there you've got me.

MISS GIRARD

No, I mean what's your job? Like Frank here is Executive Officer.

ROBERTS

Oh, I'm just the Laundry and Morale Officer.

MISS GIRARD

Why, that's wonderful—I've just been made Laundry and Morale Officer in our outfit!

PULVER

Oh, for Christ's sake!
(MANNION and INSIGNA *begin an argument in whispers.*)

MISS GIRARD

Maybe we can get together and compare notes.

ROBERTS

I'd enjoy that very much.

PULVER

(*Attempting to usher* MISS GIRARD *off*)
Look, Doug. Will you excuse us? We're going down to have a little drink.

MISS GIRARD

Frank, I don't think that's very nice. Aren't you going to ask Doug to join us?

PULVER

Hell, no—I mean—he doesn't like Scotch.

ROBERTS

That's right, Miss Girard. I stay true to alcohol and orange juice.

70

PULVER

Come on, Ann . . .

MISS GIRARD

Wait a minute! A lot of the girls at the hospital swear by alcohol and orange juice. We ought to all get together and have a party in our new dayroom.

INSIGNA

(*To* MANNION)

I bet you fifty bucks . . .

(STEFANOWSKI *moves* INSIGNA *and* MANNION *away from* MISS GIRARD.)

MISS GIRARD

Seems to be an argument.

PULVER

Yeah.

MISS GIRARD

Well, anyhow, we're fixing up a new dayroom. (*She looks offstage*) Look, you can see it! The hospital! And there's our new dormitory! That first window . . .

(PULVER *takes glasses from* WILEY *to look at island.*)

INSIGNA

(*To* MANNION, *his voice rising*)

All right, I got a *hundred* bucks says that's the one with the birthmark on her ass.

(*There is a terrible silence.* MISS GIRARD, *after a moment, takes the glasses from* PULVER *and looks at the island. After a moment she lowers the glasses and speaks to* PULVER.)

MISS GIRARD

Frank, I won't be able to have lunch with you after all.

71

Would you call the boat, please? (*To* ROBERTS) Good-bye, Doug. It was nice knowing you. You see, I promised the girls I'd help them hang some curtains and I think we'd better get started right away. Good-bye, everybody. (*To* MANNION) Oh, what's your name again?

INSIGNA

Mine?

MISS GIRARD

No. Yours.

MANNION

Mine? (MISS GIRARD *nods*) Mannion.

MISS GIRARD

Well, Mannion. I wouldn't take that bet if I were you because you'd lose a hundred bucks. (*To* PULVER) Come on, Harmless.

(*She exits, followed by a bewildered* PULVER. *The men watch her off.* STEFANOWSKI *throws his cap on the ground in anger.*)

MANNION

(*To* INSIGNA)

You loud-mouthed little bastard! Now you've gone and done it!

ROBERTS

Shut up! Insigna, how did you . . .

INSIGNA

We seen her taking a bath.

LINDSTROM

Through these glasses, Mister Roberts! We could see everything!

72

STEFANOWSKI
(*Furious*)
You heard what she said—she's going to hang some curtains.

MANNION
Yeah . . .

LINDSTROM
Gee, them nurses was pretty to look at.
(*He sighs. There is a little tragic moment.*)

ROBERTS
She's got a ten-minute boat ride. You've still got ten minutes.

WILEY
It wouldn't be any fun when you know you're going to be rushed.

LINDSTROM
This was the first real good day this ship has ever had. But it's all over now.

ROBERTS
Well, maybe you've got time then to listen to a little piece of news . . . (*He reads from the paper in his hands*) "When in all respects ready for sea, on or about 1600 today, the *AK 601* will proceed at ten knots via points X-Ray, Yolk and Zebra to Elysium Island, arriving there in seven days and reporting to the Port Director for cargo assignment." (*Emphatically*) "During its stay in Elysium, the ship will make maximum use of the recreational facilities of this port."
(*The men look up in slow surprise and disbelief.*)

STEFANOWSKI
But that means liberty!

73

LINDSTROM

That don't mean liberty, Mister Roberts?

ROBERTS

That's exactly what it means!

INSIGNA

(*Dazed*)

Somebody must've been drunk to send us to a Liberty Port!
(ROBERTS *nods*.)

LINDSTROM

Has the Old Man seen them orders?

ROBERTS

He saw them before I did.
(*Now the men are excited*.)

WILEY

Elysium! Where's that?

MANNION

Yeah! Where's that, Mister Roberts?
(*The men crowd around* ROBERTS *as he sits on the hatch*.)

ROBERTS

(*Reading from guide-book*)

"Elysium is the largest of the Limbo Islands. It is often re-
ferred to as the 'Polynesian Paradise.' Vanilla, sugar, cocoa,
coffee, copra, mother-of-pearl, phosphates and rum are the
chief exports."

INSIGNA

Rum! Did you hear that?
(*He gooses* LINDSTROM.)

74

LINDSTROM

Cut that out!

(DOLAN *gooses* INSIGNA.)

INSIGNA

Cut that out!

MANNION

Shut up!

ROBERTS

"Elysium City, its capital, is a beautiful metropolis of palm-lined boulevards, handsome public buildings and colorful stucco homes. Since 1900, its population has remained remarkably constant at approximately 30,000.

INSIGNA

I'll fix that!

(*The men shout him down.*)

ROBERTS

That's all there is here. If you want the real dope on Elysium, there's one man on this ship who's been there.

STEFANOWSKI

Who's that?

MANNION

Who?

ROBERTS

Dowdy!

The men run off wildly in every direction, shouting for DOWDY. *The call is taken up all over the ship.* ROBERTS *listens to them happily, then notices a pair of binoculars. He looks toward the island for a moment, shrugs and is lifting the binoculars to his eyes as the lights*

Fade Out

75

Scene V

During the darkness we can hear the exciting strains of Polynesian music.

The lights come up slowly through a porthole, casting a strong late-afternoon shaft of light onto motionless white figures. It is the enlisted men's compartment below decks. Except for a few not yet fully dressed, the men are all in white uniforms. The compartment is a crowded place with three-tiered bunks against the bulkheads. Most of the men are crowded around the porthole, downstage left. The men who cannot see are listening to the reports of INSIGNA, *who is standing on a bench, looking out the porthole. The only man who is not galvanized with excitement is* DOWDY, *who sits calmly on a bench, downstage center, reading a magazine—*True Detective.

GERHART

(*To* INSIGNA)

What do you see now, Sam?

INSIGNA

There's a lot of little boats up forward—up around the bow.

PAYNE

What kind of boats?

INSIGNA

They're little sort of canoes and they're all filled up with flowers and stuff. And there's women in them boats, paddling them . . .

76

PAYNE

Are they coming down this way?

INSIGNA

Naw. They're sticking around the bow.

STEFANOWSKI

Sam, where's that music coming from?

INSIGNA

There's a great big canoe up there and it's all filled with fat
bastards with flowers in their ears playing little old git-tars . . .

SCHLEMMER

Why the hell can't we go up on deck? That's what I'd like
to know!

LINDSTROM

When are we going ashore! That's what I'd like to know!
(INSIGNA *suddenly laughs.*)

PAYNE

What is it, Sam?

INSIGNA

I wish you could see this . . .
(CHIEF JOHNSON *enters, looking knowingly at the men,
shakes his head and addresses* DOWDY.)

JOHNSON

Same story in here, eh? Every porthole this side of the ship!

DOWDY

They're going to wear themselves down to a nub before they
ever get over there . . .

77

LINDSTROM

(*Takes coin from pocket and thrusts it at* INSIGNA)

Hey, Sam, here's another penny. Make them kids down below dive for it.

INSIGNA

(*Impatiently*)

All right! (*Throws coin out the port*) Heads up, you little bastards!

(*The men watch tensely.*)

LINDSTROM

Did he get that one too?

INSIGNA

Yeah . . .

(*The men relax somewhat.*)

LINDSTROM

Them kids don't ever miss!

INSIGNA

Hey, Dowdy—where's that little park again? Where you said all the good-looking women hang out?

DOWDY

For the last time—you see that big hill over there to the right . . .

INSIGNA

Yeah.

DOWDY

You see a big church . . . with a street running off to the left of it.

78

INSIGNA

Yeah.

DOWDY

Well, you go up that street three blocks . . .

INSIGNA

Yeah, I'm there.

DOWDY

That's the park.

INSIGNA

Well, I'll be damned . . .

LINDSTROM

Hey, show me that park, Sam?

(*The other men gather around* INSIGNA, *asking to see the park.*)

INSIGNA

(*The authority now*)

All right, you bastards, line up. I'll show you where the women hang out.

(*The men form a line and each steps up to the porthole where* INSIGNA *points out the park.*)

JOHNSON

(*To* DOWDY)

Smell that shoe polish? These guys have gone nuts!

DOWDY

I went down the ship's store the other day to buy a bar of soap and, do you know, they been sold out for a week! No soap, no Listerine, no lilac shaving lotion—hell, they even sold eighteen jars of Mum! Now these bastards are bootlegging it! They're gettin' ten bucks for a used jar of Mum!

79

(REBER, *wearing the messenger's belt, enters. The men greet him excitedly.*)

STEFANOWSKI

What's the word on liberty, Reber? Is the Old Man still asleep?

MANNION

Yeah, what's the word?

REBER

I just peeked in on him. He's snoring like a baby.

GERHART

Jeez, how any guy can sleep at a time like this!

INSIGNA

I'll get him up! I'm going up there and tap on his door! (*Picks up a heavy lead pipe.*)

DOWDY

(*Grabbing* INSIGNA)

Like hell you are! You're going to stay right here and pray. You're going to pray that he wakes up feeling good and decides he's kept you guys sweating long enough!

MANNION

That's telling the little crud! (INSIGNA *and* MANNION *threaten each other.*)

REBER

Hey, Lindstrom. I got good news for you. You can take them whites off.

LINDSTROM

I ain't got the duty *tonight?*

REBER

That's right. You and Mister Roberts got the duty tonight—
the twelve to four watch. The Exec just posted the list . . .
> (*He is interrupted by the sound of static on the squawk
> box. Instantly all men turn toward it eagerly.*)

DOLAN
> (*On squawk box*)

Now hear this! Now hear this!

WILEY

Here we go! Here we go!

STEFANOWSKI
> (*Imitating the squawk box*)

Liberty . . . will com-mence . . . immediately!

GERHART

Quiet!

DOLAN
> (*On squawk box*)

Now hear this! The Captain's messenger will report to the
Captain's cabin on the double!

REBER

My God! He's awake!
> (*He runs out.*)

PAYNE

Won't be long now!

WILEY

Get going, Mannion! Get into those whites! We're going to be the first ones over the side!

MANNION

Hell, yes! Give me a hand!
(*Now there is a general frenzy of preparation—the men put the last-minute touches to shoes, hair, uniforms.*)

GERHART

(*Singing to the tune of "California, Here I Come"*)
Ee-liss-*ee*-um, here I come! . . .
Ta-ta-ta-ta-*ta*-da-tah . . .

SCHLEMMER

(*To* GERHART)
Watch where you're going! You stepped on my shine!

INSIGNA

Schlemmer . . . Stef . . . Gerhart . . . come here! (*These men gather around him.* LINDSTROM *remains unhappily alone*) Now listen! Stefanowski and me are going to work alone for the first hour and a half! But if you pick up something first . . . (*Produces small map from his pocket*) We'll be working up and down this street here . . .
(*They study the map. Now the squawk box is clicked on again. All the men stand rigid, listening.*)

DOLAN

(*On squawk box*)
Now hear this! Now hear this! The Captain is now going to make a personal announcement.
(*Sound of squawk-box switch.*)

CAPTAIN

(*On squawk box*)

Goddammit, how does this thing work? (*Sound of squawk-box switch again*) This is the Captain speaking. I just woke up from a little nap and I got a surprise. I found out there were men on this ship who were expecting liberty. (*At this point, the lights start dimming until the entire scene is blacked out. The speech continues throughout the darkness. Under the* CAPTAIN's *speech the strains of Polynesian music can be heard*) Now I don't know how such a rumor got around, but I'd like to clear it up right now. You see, it's like this. Because of cargo requirements and security conditions which has just come to my personal attention there will be no liberty as long as we're in this here port. And one other thing—as long as we're here, no man will wear white uniforms. Now I would like to repeat for the benefit of complete understanding and clearness, NO LIBERTY. That is all.

Scene VI

The lights come up on the CAPTAIN's *cabin. Against the left bulkhead is a settee. A chair is placed center. Up center is the only door. The* CAPTAIN *is seated behind his desk, holding a watch in one hand and the microphone in the other, in an attitude of waiting. Just over the desk and against the right bulkhead is a ship's intercommunication board. There is a wall-safe in the right bulkhead. After a moment there is a knock on the door.*

CAPTAIN

Come in, Mister Roberts. (*As* ROBERTS *enters, the* CAPTAIN *puts the microphone on the desk*) Thirty-eight seconds. Pretty good time! You see, I been expectin' you ever since I made my little announcement.

ROBERTS

Well, as long as you're expecting me, what about it—when does this crew get liberty?

CAPTAIN

Well, in the first place, just kinda hold your tongue. And in the second place, sit down.

ROBERTS

There's no time to sit down. When are you going to let this crew go ashore?

84

CAPTAIN

I'm not. This wasn't my idea—coming to a Liberty Port. One of my officers arranged it with a certain Port Director—gave him a bottle of Scotch whiskey—compliments of the Captain. And the Port Director was kind enough to send me a little thank-you note along with our orders. Sit down, Mister Roberts. (ROBERTS *sits*) Don't worry about it. I'm not going to make trouble about that wasted bottle of Scotch. I'll admit I was a little pre-voked about not being consulted. Then I got to thinking maybe we oughta come to this port anyway so's you and me could have a little talk.

ROBERTS

You can make all the trouble you want, Captain, but let's quit wasting time. Don't you hear that music? Don't you know it's tearing those guys apart? They're breakable, Captain! I promise you!

CAPTAIN

That's enough! I've had enough of your fancy educated talk. (*Rises, goes to* ROBERTS) Now you listen to me. I got two things I want to show you. (*He unlocks the wall-safe, opens it and takes out a commander's cap with gold braid "scrambled eggs" on the visor*) You see that? That's the cap of a full commander. I'm gonna wear that cap some day and you're going to help me. (*Replaces cap in safe, goes back to* ROBERTS) I guess there's no harm in telling you that you helped me get that palm tree by working cargo. Now don't let this go to your head, but when Admiral Finchley gave me that award, he said, "You got a good Cargo Officer, Morton; keep him at it, you're going places." So I went out and bought that hat. There's nothing gonna stand between me and that hat—certainly not you. Now last week you wrote a letter that said "disharmony aboard this ship." I told you there wasn't going to be any more

85

letters. But what do I find on my desk this morning . . . (*Taking letter from desk*) Another one. It says "friction between myself and the Commanding Officer." That ain't gonna go in, Mister.

ROBERTS

How are you going to stop it, Captain?

CAPTAIN

I ain't, you are. (*Goes to his chair and sits*) Just how much do you want this crew to have a liberty anyhow? Enough to stop this "disharmony"? To stop this "friction"? (*Leans forward*) Enough to get out of the habit of writing letters ever? Because that's the only way this crew is ever gonna get ashore. (*Leans back*) Well, we've had our little talk. What do you say?

ROBERTS
(*After a moment*)

How did you get in the Navy? How did you get on our side? You're what I joined to fight *against*. You ignorant, arrogant, ambitious . . . (*Rises*) jackass! Keeping a hundred and sixty-seven men in prison because you got a palm tree for the work *they* did. I don't know which I hate worse—you or that other malignant growth that stands outside your door!

CAPTAIN

Why, you goddamn . . .

ROBERTS

How did you ever get command of a ship? I realize that in wartime they have to scrape the bottom of the barrel, but where the hell did they ever scrape you up?

CAPTAIN

(*Shouting*)

There's just one thing left for you, by God—a general court-martial.

ROBERTS

That suits me fine. Court-martial me!

CAPTAIN

By God, you've got it!

ROBERTS

I'm asking for it!

CAPTAIN

You don't have to ask for it, you've got it now!

ROBERTS

If I can't get transferred off here, I'll get court-martialed off! I'm fed up! But you'll need a witness. Send for your messenger. He's down below. I'll say it all again in front of him. (*Pauses*) Go on, call in Reber! (*The* CAPTAIN *doesn't move*) Go on, call him. (*Still the* CAPTAIN *doesn't move*) Do you want me to call him?

CAPTAIN

No. (*He walks upstage, then turns to* ROBERTS) I think you're a pretty smart boy. I may not talk very good, Mister, but I know how to take care of smart boys. Let me tell you something. Let me tell you a little secret. I hate your guts, you college son-of-a-bitch! You think you're better than I am! You think you're better because you've had everything handed to you! Let me tell you something, Mister—I've worked since I was ten years old, and all my life I've known you superior bastards. I knew you people when I was a kid in Boston and I worked in eating-places and you ordered me around. . . . "Oh, bus-boy! My friend here seems to have thrown up on

87

the table. Clean it up, please." I started going to sea as a steward and I worked for you then . . . "Steward, take my magazine out to the deck chair!" . . . "Steward, I don't like your looks. Please keep out of my way as much as possible!" Well, I took that crap! I took that for years from pimple-faced bastards who weren't good enough to wipe my nose! And now I don't have to take it any more! There's a war on, by God, and I'm the Captain and you can wipe my nose! The worst thing I can do to you is to keep you on this ship! And that's where you're going to stay! Now get out of here!

(*He goes to his chair and sits.* ROBERTS *moves slowly toward the door. He hears the music, goes to the port-hole and listens. Then he turns to the* CAPTAIN.)

ROBERTS

Can't you hear that music, Captain?

CAPTAIN

Yeah, I hear it.

(*Busies himself at desk, ignoring* ROBERTS.)

ROBERTS

Don't you know those guys below can hear it too? Oh, my God.

CAPTAIN

Get out of here.

(*After a moment,* ROBERTS *turns from the porthole and slumps against the* CAPTAIN's *locker. His face is strained.*)

ROBERTS

What do you want for liberty, Captain?

CAPTAIN

I want plenty. You're through writin' letters—ever.

88

ROBERTS

Okay.

CAPTAIN

That's not all. You're through givin' me trouble. You're through talkin' back to me in front of the crew. You ain't even gonna open your mouth—except in civil answer. (ROBERTS *doesn't answer*) Mister Roberts, you know that if you don't take my terms I'll let you go out that door and that's the end of any hope for liberty.

ROBERTS

Is that all, Captain?

CAPTAIN

No. Anyone know you're in here?

ROBERTS

No one.

CAPTAIN

Then you won't go blabbin' about this to anyone ever. It might not sound so good. And besides I don't want you to take credit for gettin' this crew ashore.

ROBERTS

Do you think I'm doing this for credit? Do you think I'd *let* anyone know about this?

CAPTAIN

I gotta be sure.

ROBERTS

You've got my word, that's all.

CAPTAIN
(*After a pause*)

Your word. Yes, you college fellas make a big show about keeping your word.

89

ROBERTS

How about it, Captain. Is it a deal?

CAPTAIN

Yeah. (ROBERTS *picks up the microphone, turns on a switch and thrusts the microphone at the* CAPTAIN) Now hear this. This is the Captain speaking. I've got some further word on security conditions in this port and so it gives me great pleasure to tell you that liberty, for the starboard section . . .

ROBERTS

(*Covering the microphone with his hand*)
For the entire crew, goddammit.

CAPTAIN

Correction: Liberty for the entire crew will commence immediately.
(ROBERTS *turns off the microphone. After a moment we hear the shouts of the crew.* ROBERTS *goes up to porthole. The* CAPTAIN *leans back on his chair. A song, "Roll Me Over," is started by someone and is soon taken up by the whole crew.*)

ROBERTS

(*Looking out of the porthole. He is excited and happy*)
Listen to those crazy bastards. Listen to them.
(*The crew continues to sing with increasing volume. Now the words can be distinguished:*
Roll me over in the clover,
Roll me over, lay me down
And do it again.)

The Curtain Falls

ACT TWO

ACT TWO

Scene I

The curtain rises on the main set. It is now 3:45 A.M. The night is pitch-black, but we can see because of a light over the head of the gangway, where a temporary desk has been rigged; a large ship's logbook lies open on this desk. A small table on which are hospital supplies is at left of the door.

At rise, ROBERTS, DOC, LINDSTROM, JOHNSON *and four* SEAMEN *are discovered onstage.* LINDSTROM, *in web belt, is writing in the log.* ROBERTS *is standing with a pile of yellow slips in his hand; he wears the side-arms of the Officer of the Deck.* JOHNSON *and a* SEAMAN *are standing near the hatchway, holding the inert body of another* SEAMAN, *who has court plaster on his face. Two more* SEAMEN *lie on the hatch cover where* DOC *is kneeling, bandaging one of them. As the curtain rises we hear the sound of a siren off right. Everyone turns and looks—that is, everyone who is conscious.*

LINDSTROM

Here's another batch, Mister Roberts—a whole paddy wagon full. And this one's an Army paddy wagon.

ROBERTS

We haven't filed away this batch yet. (*To* DOC) Hurry up, Doc.

93

JOHNSON

(*To* DOC, *indicating body he is carrying*)

Where do we put number twenty-three here, Doc? Sick bay or what?

DOC

Just put him to bed. His condition's only critical.

JOHNSON

(*Carrying* SEAMAN *off*)

They just roll out of their bunks, Doc. Now I'm stacking 'em on the deck down there—I'm on the third layer already.

VOICE

(*Offstage*)

Okay, Lieutenant! All set down here! You ready?

ROBERTS

(*Calling offstage—and giving hand signal*)

Okay! (*To* DOC) Here they come, Doc! Heads up!

SHORE PATROLMAN'S VOICE

(*Offstage*)

Lieutenant!

ROBERTS

Oh, not you again!

SHORE PATROLMAN'S VOICE

(*Offstage*)

I got a bunch of real beauties for you this time.

ROBERTS

(*Calling offstage*)

Can they walk?

94

SHORE PATROLMAN'S VOICE
(*Offstage*)

Just barely!

ROBERTS
(*Calling*)

Then send 'em up.

LINDSTROM

Man, oh, man, what a liberty! We got the record now,
Mister Roberts! This makes the seventh batch since we went
on watch!
(*The sound of a cargo winch and a voice offstage singing the Army Air Corps song are heard.* ROBERTS *is looking offstage.*)

ROBERTS
(*Signaling*)

Looks like a real haul this time. Schlemmer, look out!

LINDSTROM

Schlemmer, look out!

ROBERTS

Okay, Doc.
(DOC *and* ROBERTS *lift the two bodies from the hatch
cover and deposit them farther upstage. At this moment, the cargo net appears, loaded with bodies in once-
white uniforms and leis. Riding on top of the net is*
SCHLEMMER, *wearing a lei and singing "Off We Go into
the Wild Blue Yonder."*)

Let her in easy . . .

LINDSTROM

Let her in easy . . .
(*The net is lowered onto the hatch cover and* LINDSTROM
detaches it from the hook. All start untangling bodies.)

95

ROBERTS

Well, they're peaceful anyhow.

(*At this point a* SHORE PATROLMAN *enters from the gangway*.)

SHORE PATROLMAN

(*Handing* ROBERTS *a sheaf of yellow slips*)

For your collection. (*Points down gangway*) Take a look at them.

ROBERTS

(*Looks offstage*)

My God, what did they do?

SHORE PATROLMAN

They done all right, Lieutenant. Six of them busted into a formal dance and took on a hundred and twenty-eight Army bastards. (*Calls off*) All right, let's go!

(STEFANOWSKI, REBER, WILEY, PAYNE *and* MANNION, *with his arm around* INSIGNA, *straggle on—a frightening sight—followed by a* MILITARY POLICEMAN. INSIGNA'S *uniform is torn to shreds.* MANNION *is clad in a little diaper of crepe paper. All have bloody faces and uniforms. A few bear souvenirs—a Japanese lantern, leis, Army caps, a Shore Patrol band, etc. They throw perfunctory salutes to the colors, then murmur a greeting to* ROBERTS.)

MILITARY POLICEMAN

Duty Officer?

ROBERTS

That's right.

MILITARY POLICEMAN

(*Salutes*)

Colonel Middleton presents his compliments to the Captain and wishes him to know that these men made a shambles out of the Colonel's testimonial dinner-dance.

ROBERTS

Is this true, Insigna?

INSIGNA

That's right, Mister Roberts. A shambles. (*To* MANNION) Ain't that right, Killer?

MANNION

That's right, Mister Roberts.

ROBERTS

You men crashed a dance for Army personnel?

MANNION

Yes, sir! And they made us feel unwelcome! (*To* INSIGNA) Didn't they, Slugger?

ROBERTS

Oh, they started a fight, eh?

WILEY

No, sir! *We* started it!

STEFANOWSKI

We finished it too! (*To* MILITARY POLICEMAN) Tell Mister Roberts how many of you Army bastards are in the hospital.

MANNION

Go on.

MILITARY POLICEMAN

Thirty-eight soldiers of the United States Army have been hospitalized. And the Colonel himself has a very bad bruise on his left shin!

PAYNE

I did that, Mister Roberts.

97

MILITARY POLICEMAN

And that isn't all, Lieutenant. There were young ladies present—fifty of them. Colonel Middleton had been lining them up for a month, from the finest families of Elysium. And he had personally guaranteed their safety this evening. Well, sir . . .

ROBERTS

Well?

MILITARY POLICEMAN

Two of those young ladies got somewhat mauled, one actually got a black eye, six of them got their clothes torn off and then went screaming off into the night and they haven't been heard from since. What are you going to do about it, Lieutenant?

ROBERTS

Well, I'm due to get relieved here in fifteen minutes—I'll be glad to lead a search party.

MILITARY POLICEMAN

No, sir. The Army's taking care of that end. The Colonel will want to know what punishment you're going to give these men.

ROBERTS

Tell the Colonel that I'm sure our Captain will think of something.

MILITARY POLICEMAN

But . . .

ROBERTS

That's all, Sergeant.

MILITARY POLICEMAN
(*Salutes*)

Thank you, sir.
(*He goes off.*)

SHORE PATROLMAN

Lieutenant, I been pretty sore at your guys up till now—we had to put on ten extra Shore Patrolmen on account of this ship. But if you knew Colonel "Chicken" Middleton—well, I'd be willing to do this every night. (*To the men*) So long, fellows!

> (*The men call "So long."* SHORE PATROLMAN *exits, saluting* ROBERTS *and quarter-deck*.)

ROBERTS

Well, what've you got to say for yourselves?

STEFANOWSKI
(*After a moment*)

Okay if we go ashore again, Mister Roberts?

ROBERTS
(*To* LINDSTROM)

Is this the first time for these guys?

LINDSTROM
(*Showing log*)

Yes, sir, they got a clean record—they only been brought back once.

ROBERTS

What do you say, Doc?

> (*The men turn eagerly to* DOC.)

DOC

Anybody got a fractured skull?

MEN

No.

DOC

Okay, you pass the physical.

ROBERTS

Go down and take a shower first and get into some clothes.
(*The men rush to the hatchway.*)

STEFANOWSKI

We still got time to get back to that dance!
(*As they descend hatchway,* INSIGNA *pulls crepe paper
from around* MANNION *as he is halfway down the
hatchway.*)

ROBERTS

How you feeling, Doc?

DOC

These alcohol fumes are giving me a cheap drunk—other-
wise pretty routine. When do you get relieved, Doug?
(*Takes box from table and gestures for men to remove
table. They carry it off.*)

ROBERTS

Soon as Carney gets back from the island. Any minute now.

DOC

What are you grinning like a skunk for?

ROBERTS

Nothing. I always grin like a skunk. What have you got in
the box?

DOC

(*Descending hatchway—holding up small packet he has taken
from the box*)

Little favors from the Doc. I'm going to put one in each
man's hand and when he wakes up he'll find pinned to his

shirt full instructions for its use. I think it'll save me a lot of work later on.

(*His head disappears.*)

LINDSTROM

I wish Gerhart would get back here and relieve me. I've got to get over to that island before it runs out of women.

(DOLAN *enters from gangway.*)

DOLAN

Howdy, Mister Roberts! I'm drunk as a goat! (*Pulls a goat aboard*) Show him how drunk I am. Mister Roberts, when I first saw her she was eatin', and you know, she just eat her way into my heart. She was eatin' a little old palm tree and I thought to myself, our ship needs a mascot. (*He points out palm tree to goat*) There you are, kid. Chow!

(ROBERTS *blocks his way.*)

ROBERTS

Wait a minute . . . wait a minute. What's her name?

DOLAN

I don't know, sir.

ROBERTS

She's got a name plate.

DOLAN

Oh, so she has . . . her name is . . . (*Reads from tag on goat's collar*) . . . Property Of.

ROBERTS

What's her last name?

DOLAN

Her last name . . . (*Reads again*) Rear Admiral Wentworth.

(*Approaching siren is heard offstage.*)

ROBERTS

Okay, Dolan, hit the sack. I'll take care of her.

DOLAN

Okay, Mister Roberts. (*Descends hatchway*) See that she gets a good square meal.

(*He points to the* CAPTAIN's *palm tree and winks, then disappears.* GERHART *enters from gangway.*)

LINDSTROM

Gerhart!

(LINDSTROM *frantically removes his web belt and shoves it at* GERHART.)

GERHART

Okay, okay—you're relieved.

LINDSTROM

(*Tosses a fast salute to* ROBERTS *and says in one breath*) Requestpermissiontogoashore!

(*He hurries down gangway.*)

(SHORE PATROLMAN *enters from gangway.*)

SHORE PATROLMAN

Lieutenant, has one of your men turned up with a . . . (*Sees goat and takes leash*) Oh, thanks. (*To goat*) Come on, come on, your papa over there is worried about you.

(*Pulls goat down gangway.*)

GERHART

Where's your relief, Mister Roberts?

ROBERTS

(*Sitting on hatch*)

He'll be along any minute. How was your liberty, Gerhart?

(GERHART *grins. So does* ROBERTS. DOC *enters from hatchway.*)

DOC

What are you looking so cocky about anyway?

ROBERTS

Am I looking cocky? Maybe it's because for the first time since I've been on this ship, I'm seeing a crew.

DOC

What do you think you've been living with all this time?

ROBERTS

Just a hundred and sixty-seven separate guys. There's a big difference, Doc. Now these guys are bound together. You saw Insigna and Mannion. Doc, I think these guys are strong enough now to take all the miserable, endless days ahead of us. I only hope I'm strong enough.

DOC

Doug, tomorrow you and I are going over there and take advantage of the groundwork that's been laid tonight. You and I are going to have ourselves a liberty.

(PULVER *enters slowly from the gangway and walks across the stage.* DOC *calls* ROBERTS' *attention to him.*)

ROBERTS

Hello, Frank. How was your liberty?

(PULVER *half turns, shrugs and holds up seven fingers, then exits. A* SHORE PATROL OFFICER *enters from the gangway and calls offstage. He speaks with a Southern accent.*)

SHORE PATROL OFFICER

That's your post and that's your post. You know what to do. (*He salutes the quarter-deck, then* ROBERTS) Officer of the Deck? (ROBERTS *nods. The* SHORE PATROL OFFICER *hesitates a moment*) I hope you don't mind but I've stationed two of my men at the foot of the gangway. I'm sorry but this ship is restricted for the rest of its stay in Elysium. Your Captain is to report to the Island Commander at seven o'clock this morning. I'd recommend that he's there on time. The Admiral's a pretty tough cookie when he's mad, and he's madder now than I've ever seen him.

ROBERTS

What in particular did this?

SHORE PATROL LIEUTENANT

A little while ago six men from your ship broke into the home of the French Consul and started throwing things through the plate-glass living-room window. We found some of the things on the lawn: a large world globe, a small love seat, a lot of books and a bust of Balzac—the French writer. We also found an Army private first class who was unconscious at the time. He claims they threw him too.

ROBERTS

Through the window?

MISTER ROBERTS

SHORE PATROL LIEUTENANT

That's right! It seems he took them there for a little joke. He didn't tell them it was the Consul's house; he said it was a—what we call in Alabama—a cat-house. (ROBERTS *and* DOC *nod*) Be sure that your Captain is there at seven o'clock sharp. If it makes you feel any better, Admiral Wentworth says this is the worst ship he's ever seen in his entire naval career. (*Laughs, then salutes*) Good night, Lieutenant.

ROBERTS
(*Returning salute*)

Good night.
    (*The* SHORE PATROL LIEUTENANT *exits down gangway—saluting the quarter-deck.*)

GERHART

Well, there goes the liberty. That was sure a wham-bam-thank you, ma'am!

DOC

Good night.
    (*He exits through left passageway.*)

GERHART

But, by God, it was worth it. That liberty was worth anything!

ROBERTS

I think you're right, Gerhart.

GERHART

Hunh?

ROBERTS

I think you're right.

GERHART

Yeah.

He smiles. ROBERTS *looks over the log.* GERHART *whistles
softly to himself "Roll Me Over" as the lights slowly*

Fade Out

During the darkness we hear JOHNSON *shouting:*

JOHNSON

All right, fall in for muster. Form two ranks. And pipe
down.

Scene II

The lights come up, revealing the deck. Morning sunlight. A group of men, right and left, in orderly formation. They are talking.

JOHNSON

'Ten-shun!
> (*The command is relayed through the ship. The* CAP-
> TAIN *enters from his cabin, followed by* ROBERTS. *The*
> CAPTAIN *steps up on the hatch cover.* ROBERTS *starts to*
> *fall in with the men.*)

CAPTAIN

(*Calling to* ROBERTS *and pointing to a place beside himself on hatch cover*)

Over here, Roberts. (ROBERTS *takes his place left of* CAPTAIN) We're being kicked out of this port. I had a feeling this liberty was a bad idea. That's why we'll never have one again. We're going to erase this blot from my record if we have to work twenty-four hours a day. We're going to move even more cargo than we've ever moved before. And if there ain't enough cargo work, Mister Roberts here is gonna find some. Isn't that right, Mister Roberts? (ROBERTS *doesn't answer*) Isn't that right, Mister Roberts?

ROBERTS

Yes, sir.

CAPTAIN

I'm appointing Mister Roberts here and now to see that you men toe the line. And I can't think of a more honorable

108

man for the job. He's a man who keeps his word no matter what. (*Turns to* ROBERTS) Now, Roberts, if you do a good job —and if the Admiral begins to smile on us again—there might be something in it for you. What would you say if that little silver bar on your collar got a twin brother some day? (ROBERTS *is startled. The* CAPTAIN *calls offstage*) Officer of the Deck!

OFFSTAGE VOICE

Yes, sir!

CAPTAIN
(*To* ROBERTS)

You wasn't expectin' that, was you? (*Calling offstage*) Get ready to sail!

OFFSTAGE VOICE

Aye-aye, sir!

CAPTAIN

You men are dismissed!

JOHNSON

Fall out!
(*The men fall out. Some exit. A little group forms downstage.*)

CAPTAIN

Wait a minute! Wait a minute! Roberts, take these men here back aft to handle lines. And see that they work up a sweat. (ROBERTS *and men look at him*) Did you hear me, Roberts? I gave you an order!

ROBERTS
(*Carefully*)

Yes, Captain. I heard you.

CAPTAIN

How do you answer when I give an order?

ROBERTS

(*After a pause*)

Aye-aye, sir.

CAPTAIN

That's more like it . . . that's more like it!
(*He exits into his cabin.*)

STEFANOWSKI

What'd he mean, Mister Roberts?

ROBERTS

I don't know. Just what he said, I guess.

GERHART

What'd you let him give you all that guff for?

DOLAN

(*Stepping up on hatch, carrying a file folder*)

Because he's tired, that's why. He had the mid-watch last night. Your tail'd be dragging too if you had to handle all them customers.

ROBERTS

Come on. Let's get going . . .

DOLAN

Wait a minute, Mister Roberts. Something come for you in the mail this morning—a little love letter from the Bureau. (*Pulls out paper from file folder*) Get a load of this! (*Reads*) "To All Ships and Stations: Heightened war offensive has created urgent need aboard combat ships for experienced officers. (*He clicks his teeth and winks at* ROBERTS) All commanding officers are hereby directed to forward with their endorsements all applications for transfer from officers with twenty-four months' sea duty." (ROBERTS *grabs the directive and reads it.* DOLAN *looks at* ROBERTS *and smiles*) You got twenty-nine months—you're the only officer aboard that has. Mister Roberts, the Old Man is hanging on the ropes from the working-over the Admiral give him. All he needs to flatten him is one more little jab. And here it is. Your letter. I typed it up. (*He pulls out triplicate letter from file cover—then a fountain pen which he offers to* ROBERTS) Sign it and I'll take it in—

MANNION

Go on, sign it, Mister Roberts. He'll take off like a bird.

DOLAN

What're you waitin' for, Mister Roberts?

ROBERTS

(*Handing directive back to* DOLAN)

I'll want to look it over first, Dolan. Come on, let's get going.

DOLAN

There's nothing to look over. This is the same letter we wrote yesterday—only quoting this new directive.

ROBERTS

Look, Dolan, I'm tired. And I told you I wanted—

DOLAN

You ain't too tired to sign your name!

ROBERTS
(*Sharply*)
Take it easy, Dolan. I'm not going to sign it. So take it easy! (*Turns to exit right, finds himself blocked by crew*) Did you hear me? Let's get going!
(*Exits.*)

STEFANOWSKI
What the hell's come over him?
(*They look at one another.*)

INSIGNA
Aye-aye, sir—for Christ's sake!

MANNION
(*After a moment*)
Come on. Let's get going.

DOLAN
(*Bitterly*)
"Take it easy . . . take it easy!"
The men start to move off slowly as the lights

Fade Out

During the darkness we hear a radio. There is considerable static.

AMERICAN BROADCASTER

Still, of course, we have no official word from the Headquarters of the Supreme Allied Command in Europe. I repeat, there is no official announcement yet. The report that the war in Europe has ended has come from only one correspondent. It has not been confirmed by other correspondents or by SHAEF headquarters. But here is one highly intriguing fact—that report has not been denied either in Washington or in SHAEF headquarters in Europe. IT HAS NOT BEEN DENIED. Right now in those places the newsmen are crowded, waiting to flash to the world the announcement of V-E Day.

Scene III

The lights come up on ROBERTS' *and* PULVER'S *cabin.* DOC, *at the desk, and* PULVER, *up in his bunk, are listening to the radio.*

PULVER

Turn that damn thing off, Doc. Has Doug ever said anything to you about wanting a promotion?

DOC

Of course not. I doubt if he's even conscious of what rank he is.

PULVER

You can say that again!

DOC

I doubt if he's even conscious of what rank he is.

PULVER

That's what I said. He doesn't even think about a promotion. The only thing he thinks about is the war news—up in the radio shack two weeks now—all day long—listening with a headset, reading all the bulletins . . . Anyone who says he's bucking for another stripe is a dirty liar.

DOC

Who says he is, Frank?

PULVER

Insigna, Mannion and some of the other guys. I heard them talking outside the porthole. They were talking loud on pur-

114

pose so I could hear them—they must've guessed I was lying
here on my bunk. What's happened to Doug anyway, Doc?

DOC

How would I know! He's spoken about ten words to me
in as many days. But I'm damn well going to find out.

PULVER

He won't talk, Doc. This morning I followed him all around
the room while he was shaving. I begged him to talk to me.
I says, "You're a fellow who needs a friend and here I am."
And I says, "What's all this trouble you're having with the
crew? You tell me and I'll fix it up like that." And then I
give him some real good advice—I says, "Keep your chin up,"
and things like that. And then do you know what he did? He
walked out of the room just as though I wasn't here.
    (*There is a knock on the door.*)

DOC

Come in.
    (DOWDY *enters.*)

DOWDY

Doc, Mister Pulver—could we see you officers a minute?

DOC

Sure.
    (GERHART *and* LINDSTROM *enter, closing the door*)
What is it?

DOWDY

Tell them what happened, Gerhart.

GERHART

Well, sir, I sure don't like to say this but . . . Mister
Roberts just put Dolan on report.

LINDSTROM

Me and Gerhart seen him.

PULVER

On report!

GERHART

Yes, sir. Tomorrow morning Dolan has to go up before the Captain—on account of Mister Roberts.

LINDSTROM

On account of Mister Roberts.

GERHART

And we was wondering if you officers could get him to take Dolan off report before . . . well, before—

DOC

Before what, Gerhart?

GERHART

Well, you see, the guys are all down in the compartment, talking about it. And they're saying some pretty rough things about Mister Roberts. Nobody just ever expected to see him put a man on report and . . .

LINDSTROM

He ain't gonna turn out to be like an officer, is he, Doc?

DOWDY

Lindstrom . . .

LINDSTROM

Oh, I didn't mean you, Doc . . . or even you, Mister Pulver!

DOC

That's all right, Lindstrom. What was this trouble with Dolan?

DOWDY

This letter business again!

GERHART

Yes, sir. Dolan was just kiddin' him about not sending in any more letters. And all of a sudden Mister Roberts turned just white and yelled, "Shut up, Dolan. Shut your goddamn mouth. I've had enough." And Dolan naturally got snotty back at him and Mister Roberts put him right on report.

LINDSTROM

Right on report.
(ROBERTS *enters.*)

PULVER

Hello, Doug boy. Aren't you listening to the war news?

DOWDY

All right, Doctor. We'll get that medical store room cleaned out tomorrow.
(DOWDY, GERHART *and* LINDSTROM *leave.*)

PULVER

We thought you were up in the radio shack.

ROBERTS

(*To* PULVER)

Don't you want to go down to the wardroom and have a cup of coffee?

PULVER

(*Jumping down from bunk*)

Sure. I'll go with you.

117

ROBERTS

I don't want any. Why don't you go ahead?

PULVER

Nah.
> (*He sits back on bunk. There is another little pause.*)

ROBERTS

Will you go on out anyway? I want to talk to Doc.

PULVER
> (*Rising and crossing to door*)

All right, I will. I'm going for a cup of coffee. (*Stops, turns and gets cap from top of locker*) No! I'm going up to the radio shack. You aren't the only one interested in the war news.
> (*He exits.*)

ROBERTS
> (*With emotion*)

Doc, transfer me, will you? (DOC *looks at him*) Transfer me to the hospital on this next island! You can do it. You don't need the Captain's approval! Just put me ashore for examination—say there's something wrong with my eyes or my feet or my head, for Christ's sake! You can trump up something!

DOC

What good would that do?

ROBERTS

Plenty! I could lie around that hospital for a couple of weeks. The ship would have sailed—I'd have missed it! I'd be off this ship. Will you do it, Doc?

DOC

Doug, why did you put Dolan on report just now?

ROBERTS

(*Angrily*)

I gave him an order and he didn't carry it out fast enough to suit me. (*Glares at* DOC, *who just studies him.* ROBERTS *rises and paces right*) No, that's not true. It was the war. I just heard the news. The war was ending and I couldn't get to it and there was Dolan giving me guff about something—and all of a sudden I hated him. I hated all of them. I was sick of the sullen bastards staring at me as though I'd sold them down the river or something. If they think I'm bucking for a promotion—if they're stupid enough to think I'd walk ten feet across the room to get anything from that Captain, then I'm through with the whole damn ungrateful mob!

DOC

Does this crew owe you something?

ROBERTS

What the hell do you mean by that?

DOC

You talk as if they did.

(ROBERTS *rises and crosses to bunk*.)

ROBERTS

(*Quietly*)

That's exactly how I'm talking. I didn't realize it but that's exactly the way I've been feeling. Oh, Jesus, that shows you how far gone I am, Doc. I've been taking something out on them. I've been blaming them for something that . . .

DOC

What, Doug? Something what? You've made some sort of an agreement with the Captain, haven't you, Doug!

ROBERTS
(*Turns*)

Agreement? I don't know what you mean. Will you transfer me, Doc?

DOC

Not a chance, Doug. I could never get away with it—you know that.

ROBERTS

Oh, my God!

PULVER
(*Offstage*)

Doug! Doc! (*Entering*) Listen to the radio, you uninformed bastards! Turn it up!

(ROBERTS *reaches over and turns up the radio. The excited voice of an announcer can be heard.*)

ANNOUNCER

. . . this broadcast to bring you a special news flash! The war is over in Europe! THE WAR IS OVER IN EUROPE! (ROB-ERTS *grasps* DOC's *arm in excitement*) Germany has surrendered unconditionally to the Allied Armies. The surrender was signed in a schoolhouse in the city of Rheims . . .

(ROBERTS *stands staring.* DOC *turns off the radio. For a moment there is silence, then:*)

DOC

I would remind you that there's still a minor skirmish here in the Pacific.

120

ROBERTS

I'll miss that one too. But to hell with me. This is the greatest day in the world. We're going to celebrate. How about it, Frank?

PULVER

Yeah, Doug. We've got to celebrate!

DOC

(*Starting to pull alcohol from waste basket*)
What'll it be—alcohol and orange juice or orange juice and alcohol?

ROBERTS

No, that's not good enough.

PULVER

Hell, no, Doc!
(*He looks expectantly at* ROBERTS.)

ROBERTS

We've got to think of something that'll lift this ship right out of the water and turn it around the other way.
(PULVER *suddenly rises to his feet.*)

PULVER

(*Shouting*)
Doug! Oh, my God, why didn't I think of this before. Doug! Doc! You're going to blow your tops when you hear the idea I got! Oh, Jesus, what a wonderful idea! It's the only thing to do. It's the only thing in the whole world to do! That's all! Doug, you said I never had any ideas. You said I never finished anything I started. Well, you're wrong—tonight you're wrong! I thought of something and I finished it.

I was going to save it for your birthday, but I'm going to give it to you tonight, because we gotta celebrate . . .

ROBERTS

(*Waves his hands in* PULVER's *face for attention*)
Wait a minute, Frank! What is it?

PULVER

A firecracker, by God. (*He reaches under his mattress and pulls out a large, wobbly firecracker which has been painted red*) We're gonna throw a firecracker under the Old Man's bunk. Bam-bam-bam! Wake up, you old son-of-a-bitch, IT'S V-E DAY!

ROBERTS
(*Rising*)

Frank!

PULVER

Look at her, Doc. Ain't it a beauty? Ain't that the greatest hand-made, hand-painted, hand-packed firecracker you ever saw?

ROBERTS
(*Smiling and taking firecracker*)
Yes, Frank. That's the most beautiful firecracker I ever saw in my life. But will it work?

PULVER

Sure it'll work. At least, I think so.

ROBERTS

Haven't you tested it? It's got to work, Frank, it's just got to work!

122

PULVER

I'll tell you what I'll do. I'll take it down to the laundry and test it—that's my laboratory, the laundry. I got all the fixings down there—powder, fuses, everything, all hid behind the soapflakes. And if this one works, I can make another one in two minutes.

ROBERTS

Okay, Frank. Take off. We'll wait for you here. (PULVER *starts off*) Be sure you got enough to make it loud. What'd you use for powder?

PULVER

Loud! This ain't a popgun. This is a firecracker. I used fulminate of mercury. I'll be right back.

(*He runs out.*)

ROBERTS

Fulminate of mercury! That stuff's murder! Do you think he means it?

DOC

(*Taking alcohol bottle from waste basket*)

Of course not. Where could he get fulminate of mercury?

ROBERTS

I don't know. He's pretty resourceful. Where did he get the clap last year?

DOC

How about a drink, Doug?

(*He pours alcohol and orange juice into two glasses.*)

ROBERTS

Right! Doc, I been living with a genius. This makes it all worth while—the whole year and a half he spent in his bunk. How else could you celebrate V-E Day? A firecracker under the Old Man's bunk! The silly little son-of-a-bitch!

123

DOC

(*Handing* ROBERTS *a drink*)

Here you are, Doug. (DOC *holds the drink up in a toast*)
To better days!

ROBERTS

Okay. And to a great American, Frank Thurlowe Pulver
. . . Soldier . . . Statesman . . . Scientist . . .

DOC

Friend of the Working Girl . . .
(*Suddenly there is a tremendous explosion.* DOC *and*
ROBERTS *clutch at the desk.*)

ROBERTS

Oh, my God!

DOC

He wasn't kidding! That's fulminate of mercury!

CAPTAIN

(*Offstage*)

What was that?
(ROBERTS *and* DOC *rush to porthole, listening.*)

JOHNSON

(*Offstage*)

I don't know, Captain. I'll find out!
(*We hear the sounds of running feet.*)

ROBERTS

Doc, we've got to go down and get him.

DOC

This may be pretty bad, Doug.

124

(*They turn to start for the door when suddenly a figure hurtles into the room and stops. For a moment it looks like a combination scarecrow and snowman but it is* PULVER—*his uniform tattered; his knees, arms and face blackened; he is covered with soapsuds and his eyes are shining with excitement.* ROBERTS *stares in amazement.*)

PULVER

Jeez, that stuff's terrific!

DOC

Are you all right?

PULVER

I'm great! Gee, you should've been there!

ROBERTS

You aren't burned—or anything?

PULVER

Hell, no. But the laundry's kinda beat up. The mangle's on the other side of the room now. And there's a new porthole on the starboard side where the electric iron went through. And I guess a steam-line must've busted or something—I was up to my ass in lather. And soapflakes flyin' around—it was absolutely beautiful!

(*During these last lines,* DOC *has been making a brisk, professional examination.*)

DOC

It's a miracle. He isn't even scratched!

PULVER

Come on down and see it, Doug. It's a Winter Wonderland!

125

CAPTAIN
(*Offstage*)

Johnson!

ROBERTS

Quiet!

JOHNSON
(*Offstage*)

Yes, sir.

CAPTAIN
(*Offstage*)

What was it?

JOHNSON
(*Offstage*)

The laundry, Captain. A steam-line must've blew up.

PULVER
(*Explaining*)

Steam-line came right out of the bulkhead. (*He demonstrates*) Whish!

CAPTAIN
(*Offstage*)

How much damage?

JOHNSON
(*Offstage*)

We can't tell yet, Captain. We can't get in there—the passageway is solid soapsuds.

PULVER

Solid soapsuds.
(*He pantomimes walking blindly through soapsuds.*)

CAPTAIN

(*Offstage*)

Tell those men to be more careful.

ROBERTS

(*Excitedly*)

Frank, our celebration is just getting started. The night is young and our duty's clear.

PULVER

Yeah? What're we gonna do now, Doug?

ROBERTS

Get cleaned up and come with me.

PULVER

Where we goin' now, Doug?

ROBERTS

We're going down and get the rest of your stuff. You proved it'd work—you just hit the wrong target, that's all. We're going to make another firecracker, and put it where it really belongs.

PULVER

(*Who has slowly wilted during* ROBERTS' *speech*)

The rest of my stuff was—in the laundry, Doug. It all went up. There isn't any more. I'm sorry, Doug. I'm awful sorry.

ROBERTS

(*Sinks into chair*)

That's all right, Frank.

PULVER

Maybe I can scrounge some more tomorrow.

ROBERTS

Sure.

PULVER

You aren't sore at me, are you, Doug?

ROBERTS

What for?

PULVER

For spoilin' our celebration?

ROBERTS

Of course not.

PULVER

It was a good idea though, wasn't it, Doug?

ROBERTS

Frank, it was a great idea. I'm proud of you. It just didn't work, that's all.

(*He starts for the door.*)

DOC

Where are you going, Doug?

ROBERTS

Out on deck.

PULVER

Wait'll I get cleaned up and I'll come with you.

ROBERTS

No, I'm going to turn in after that. (*To* PULVER) It's okay, Frank.

(*He exits.*)

(PULVER *turns pleadingly to* DOC.)

128

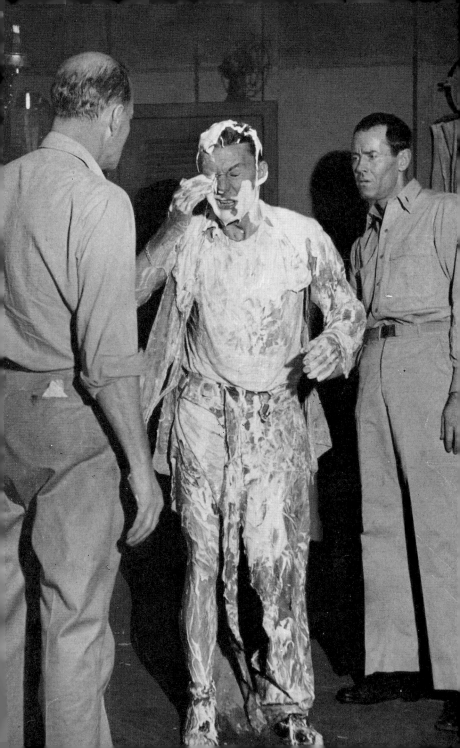

PULVER

He was happy there for a minute though, wasn't he, Doc? Did you see him laughing? He was happy as hell. (*Pause*) We gotta do something for that guy, Doc. He's in bad shape. What's the matter with him anyhow, Doc. Did you find out?

DOC

No, he wouldn't tell me. But I know one thing he's feeling tonight and that's panic. Tonight he feels his war is dying before he can get to it.

(DOC *goes to radio and turns up volume.*)

PULVER

I let him down. He wanted to celebrate and I let him down.
(*He drops his head.*)

ANNOUNCER'S VOICE *on radio comes up as the lights*

Fade Out

(During the darkness and under the first part of Scene IV we hear the voice of a British broadcaster:)

BRITISH BROADCASTER

. . . we hope that the King and the Queen will come out. The crowds are cheering—listen to them—and at any second now we hope to see Their Majesties. The color here is tremendous—everywhere rosettes, everywhere gay, red-white-and-blue hats. All the girls in their summer frocks on this lovely, mild, historic May evening. And although we celebrate with joyous heart the great victory, perhaps the greatest victory in the history of mankind, the underlying mood is a mood of thanksgiving. And now, I believe, they're coming. They haven't appeared but the crowd in the center are cheering madly. Handkerchiefs, flags, hands waving—HERE THEY COME! First, Her Majesty, the Queen, has come into view. Then the King in the uniform of an Admiral of the Fleet. The two Princesses standing on the balcony—listen to the crowd—
    (Sound of wild cheering.)

(This broadcast continues throughout the blackout and the next scene. Several times the station is changed, from a broadcast of the celebration in San Francisco to the speaker in New York and the band playing "The Stars and Stripes Forever" in Times Square.)

Scene IV

The lights dim up on the main set. It is a few minutes later, and bright moonlight. The ship is under way—this is indicated by the apparent movement of the stars, slowly up and down. A group of men are sitting on the hatch cover in a late bull session. They are INSIGNA, MANNION, DOLAN *and* STEFANOWSKI. GERHART *stands over them; he has obviously just returned from some mission for the group.*

GERHART

I'm telling you, that's all it was. A steam pipe busted in the laundry—they're cleaning it up now. It ain't worth going to see.

(*The others make way for him and he sits down beside them.* INSIGNA *cocks his head toward the sound of the radio.*)

INSIGNA

What the hell's all that jabbering on the radio now?

MANNION

I don't know. Something about the King and Queen . . .

(*The men listen for a moment without curiosity; then, as the radio fades, they settle back in indolent positions.*)

INSIGNA

Well, anyhow, like I was telling you, this big sergeant in

131

Elysium was scared to fight me! Tell 'em how big he was, Killer.

MANNION

Six foot seven or eight . . .

STEFANOWSKI

That sergeant's grown eight inches since we left Elysium . . . Did you see me when I swiped that Shore Patrol band and went around arresting guys? That Shore Patrol Lieutenant said I was the best man he had. I arrested forty-three guys . . .

MANNION
(Smiles at DOLAN who is looking depressed)
Come on, Dolan, don't let him get you down.

INSIGNA

Yeah, come on, Dolan.
(ROBERTS enters. He looks at the men, who have their backs turned, hesitates, then goes slowly over to them.)

GERHART
(Idly)
What was them croquette things we had for chow tonight?
(STEFANOWSKI looks up and notices ROBERTS. Instantly he sits upright.)

STEFANOWSKI

Flash Red!
(The men sit up. There is an embarrassed silence.)

ROBERTS

Good evening. (The men smile politely. ROBERTS is very embarrassed) Did you hear the news? The war's over in Europe.

132

MANNION
(Smiling)

Yes, sir. We heard.

STEFANOWSKI
(Helping out the conversation)
Sure. Maybe somebody'll get on the ball out here now . . .
(DOLAN *rises, starts down hatchway.*)

ROBERTS
Dolan, I guess I kind of blew my top tonight. I'm sorry. I'm taking you off report.

DOLAN
Whatever you want, sir . . . (*He looks ostentatiously at his watch and yawns*) Well, I guess I'll hit the old sack . . .
(*He goes down hatchway.*)

MANNION
Yeah, me too . . .

INSIGNA
Yeah . . .

GERHART
It's late as hell.

STEFANOWSKI
I didn't realize how late it was . . .
(*All the men get up, then go down the hatchway.* ROBERTS *stands looking after them. Now the radio is heard again.* ROBERTS *goes to hatchway and sits listening.*)

SPEAKER
. . . Our boys have won this victory today. But the rest is up to you. You and you alone must recognize our enemies: the forces of ambition, cruelty, arrogance and stupidity. You must recognize them, you must destroy them, you must tear

133

them out as you would a malignant growth! And cast them from the surface of the earth!

(The end of the speech is followed by a band playing "The Stars and Stripes Forever." ROBERTS' face lights up and a new determination is in it. He repeats the words "malignant growth." The band music swells. He marches to the palm tree, salutes it, rubs his hands together and, as the music reaches a climax, he jerks the palm tree, earth and all, from the container and throws it over the side. Then, as the music continues, loud and climactic, he brushes his hands together, shrugs, and walks casually off left singing the tune to himself.)

(For a moment the stage is empty. Then the lights go up in the CAPTAIN's cabin. The door to the CAPTAIN's cabin opens and the CAPTAIN appears. He is in pajamas and bathrobe, and in one hand he carries his watering can. He discovers the empty container. He looks at it, then plunges into his cabin. After a moment, the General Alarm is heard. It is a terrible clanging noise designed to rouse the dead. When the alarm stops, the CAPTAIN's voice is heard, almost hysterical, over the squawk box.)

CAPTAIN

General Quarters! General Quarters! Every man to his battle station on the double!

(JOHNSON, in helmet and life jacket, scurries from hatchway into the CAPTAIN's cabin. WILEY enters from right passageway and climbs into the right gun tub. Now men appear from all directions in various degrees of dress. The stage is filled with men frantically running everywhere, all wearing helmets and life preservers.)

134

INSIGNA
(Appearing from hatchway)

What happened? (*He runs up the ladder and into the left gun tub.* PAYNE *enters from left and starts to climb up to left gun tub*) Get the hell out of here, Payne. This ain't your gun—your gun's over there!

DOLAN
(Also trying to climb the ladder with PAYNE*)*

Over there . . . over there . . .

(PAYNE *crosses to right gun tub.*)

REBER
(Entering from hatchway)

What the hell happened?

SCHLEMMER

Are *we* in an air raid?

PAYNE

Submarine . . . must be a submarine!

GERHART

Hey, Wiley, what happened?

DOWDY
(Calling to someone on life raft)

Hey, get away from that life raft. He didn't say abandon ship!

(*During the confusion,* STEFANOWSKI, *bewildered, emerges from the hatchway and wanders over to right gun tub.*)

STEFANOWSKI

Hey, Wiley, Wiley—you sure you're supposed to be up there?

WILEY

Yeah.

STEFANOWSKI
(*Crossing to left gun tub*)
Hey, Sam. Are you supposed to be up there?

INSIGNA

Yeah, we was here last year!

STEFANOWSKI

Hey, Dowdy. Where the hell's my battle station?

DOWDY

I don't know where your battle station is! Look around!
(STEFANOWSKI *wanders aimlessly about.* WILEY, *in the gun tub right, is receiving reports of battle readiness from various parts of the ship:*)

WILEY

Twenty millimeters manned and ready. (*Pause*) Engine room manned and ready. (*Pause*) All battle stations manned and ready.

STEFANOWSKI
(*Sitting on corner of hatch*)
Yeah, all but mine . . .

JOHNSON'S VOICE
(*In* CAPTAIN'S *cabin*)
All battle stations manned and ready, Captain.

136

CAPTAIN'S VOICE

Give me that thing.

JOHNSON'S VOICE

(*"On mike"—that is, speaking directly into squawk-box microphone. "Off mike" means speaking unintentionally into this live microphone.*)
Attention . . . Attention . . . The Captain wishes to . . .

CAPTAIN'S VOICE
(*Off mike*)

Give me that thing! (*On mike*) All right, who did it? Who did it? You're going to stay here all night until someone confesses. You're going to stay at those battle stations until hell freezes over until I find out who did it. It's an insult to the honor of this ship, by God! The symbol of our cargo record has been destroyed and I'm going to find out who did it if it takes all night! (*Off mike*) Johnson, read me that muster list!

JOHNSON'S VOICE
(*Reading muster list off mike*)

Abernathy . . .

MANNION	CAPTAIN'S VOICE
Symbol of our cargo record? What the hell's that?	No, not Abernathy . . .
	JOHNSON'S VOICE
	Baker . . .
(STEFANOWSKI *rises, sees empty container, kneels and ceremoniously bows to it.*)	CAPTAIN'S VOICE
	No . . .
DOWDY	JOHNSON'S VOICE
For God's sake, Stefanowski, find some battle station!	Bartholomew . . . Becker . . . Billings . . .

Carney . . . Daniels . . .
Dexter . . .
Ellison . . .
Everman . . .
Jenkins . . .
Kelly . . .
Kevin . . .
Martin . . .
Olsen . . .
O'Neill . . .

(STEFANOWSKI *points to empty container.* DOWDY *sees it and spreads the news to the men on left.* SCHLEMMER *sees it and tells the other men. Now from all parts of the ship men enter and jubilantly look at the empty container. Bits of soil fly into the air as the men group around the empty can.*)

CAPTAIN'S VOICE

No, not O'Neill . . .

JOHNSON'S VOICE

Pulver . . .

CAPTAIN'S VOICE

No, not Pulver. He hasn't the guts . . .

JOHNSON'S VOICE

Roberts . . .

CAPTAIN S VOICE
(*Roaring, off mike*)
Roberts! He's the one! Get him up here!

JOHNSON'S VOICE
(*On mike*)
Mister Roberts will report to the Captain's cabin on the double!

(*The men rush back to their battle stations.*)

138

CAPTAIN'S VOICE

Get him up here, I tell you! Get him up here . . .

JOHNSON'S VOICE

(*On mike*)

Mister Roberts will report to the Captain's cabin on the . . .

CAPTAIN

(*Off mike*)

Give me that thing. (*On mike*) Roberts, you get up here in a goddamn quick hurry. Get up here! Roberts, I'm giving you an order—get the lead out of your pants.

(ROBERTS *appears from left passageway and, walking slowly, enters the* CAPTAIN's *cabin.*)

(*The men move onstage and* LINDSTROM *gets to a position on the ladder where he can look through the porthole of the* CAPTAIN's *cabin.*)

ROBERTS' VOICE

Did you want to see me, Captain?

CAPTAIN'S VOICE

You did it. You did it. Don't lie to me. Don't stand there and lie to me. Confess it!

ROBERTS' VOICE

Confess what, Captain? I don't know what you're talking about.

CAPTAIN'S VOICE

You know damn well what I'm talkin' about because you did it. You've doublecrossed me—you've gone back on your word!

ROBERTS' VOICE
No, I haven't, Captain.

CAPTAIN
Yes, by God, you have. I kept my part of the bargain! I gave this crew liberty—I gave this crew liberty, by God, but you've gone back on *your* word.

(DOWDY *takes off his helmet and looks at the men.*)

ROBERTS' VOICE
I don't see how you can say that, Captain. I haven't sent in any more letters.

(DOLAN, *on gun tub ladder, catches* INSIGNA's *eye.*)

CAPTAIN'S VOICE
I'm not talkin' about your goddamn sons-a-bitchin' letters. I'm talkin' about what you did tonight.

ROBERTS' VOICE
Tonight? I don't understand you, Captain. What do you think I did?

CAPTAIN
Quit saying that, goddammit, quit saying that. You know damn well what you did. You stabbed me in the back. You stabbed me in the back . . . aaa . . . aa . . .

JOHNSON'S VOICE
Captain! Get over to the washbasin, Captain!

CAPTAIN'S VOICE
Aaaaaaa . . .

INSIGNA
What the hell happened?

140

DOLAN

Quiet!

JOHNSON
(*On mike*)

Will the Doctor please report to the Captain's cabin on the double?

(DOC *appears from left, pushing his way through the crowd, followed by two* MEDICAL CORPSMEN *wearing Red Cross brassards and carrying first-aid kits and a stretcher.* DOC *walks slowly; he is idly attaching a brassard and smoking a cigarette. He wears his helmet sloppily.*)

DOC

Gangway . . . gangway . . .

DOWDY

Hey, Doc, tell us what's going on.

DOC

Okay. Okay.

(*He enters the* CAPTAIN's *cabin followed by the* CORPS-MEN *who leave stretcher leaning against the bulkhead. The door closes. There is a tense pause. The men gather around the cabin again.* LINDSTROM *is at the porthole.*)

REBER

Hey, Lindstrom, where's the Old Man?

LINDSTROM

He's sittin' in the chair—leaning way forward.

PAYNE

What's the Doc doin'?

LINDSTROM

He's holdin' the waste basket.

REBER

What waste basket?

LINDSTROM

The one the Old Man's got his head in. And he needs it too. (*Pause*) They're helpin' him over to the couch. (*Pause*) He's lying down there and they're takin' off his shoes. (*Pause*) Look out, here they come.

> (*The men break quickly and rush back to their battle stations. The door opens and* ROBERTS, DOC *and the* CORPSMEN *come out.*)

DOC

(*To* CORPSMEN)

We won't need that stretcher. Sorry. (*Calls*) Dowdy! Come here.

> (DOWDY *comes down to* DOC. *He avoids* ROBERTS' *eyes.*)

ROBERTS

Dowdy, pass the word to the crew to secure from General Quarters.

DOC

And tell the men not to make any noise while they go to their bunks. The Captain's resting quietly now, and I think that's desirable.

ROBERTS

Pass the word, will you, Dowdy?

DOWDY

Yes, Mister Roberts.

> (*He passes the word to the crew who slowly start to leave their battle stations. They are obviously stalling.*)

MISTER ROBERTS

DOC

(*To* ROBERTS)

Got a cigarette? (ROBERTS *reaches in his pocket and offers* DOC *a cigarette. Then he lights* DOC's *cigarette.* DOC *notices the men stalling*) Well, guess I'd better get back inside. I'll be down to see you after I get through.

> (*He enters cabin and stands there watching. The men move offstage, very slowly, saying "Good night, Mister Roberts," "Good night, sir." Suddenly* ROBERTS *notices that all the men are saying good night to him.*)

DOLAN

(*Quietly*)

Good night, Mister Roberts. (ROBERTS *does not hear him*) Good night, Mister Roberts.

ROBERTS

Good night, Dolan.

> DOLAN *smiles and exits down hatch.* ROBERTS *steps toward hatch, removes helmet, looks puzzled as the lights*

Fade Out

(During the darkness, over the squawk box the following announcements are heard:)

FIRST VOICE

Now hear this . . . Now hear this . . . C, E and S Divisions and all Pharmacist's Mates will air bedding today—positively!

SECOND VOICE

There is now available at the ship's store a small supply of peanut brittle. Ship's store will be open from 1300 to 1315.

THIRD VOICE

Now, Dolan, Yeoman Second Class, report to the radio shack immediately.

Scene V

The lights come up on the stateroom of ROBERTS *and* PULVER. PULVER *is lying in the lower bunk.* DOC *is sitting at the desk with a glass and a bottle of grain alcohol in front of him.* ROBERTS *is tying up a sea bag. A small suitcase stands beside it. His locker is open and empty.* WILEY *picks up the sea bag.*

WILEY

Okay, Mister Roberts. I'll take these down to the gangway. The boat from the island should be out here any minute for you. I'll let you know.

ROBERTS

Thanks, Wiley.

WILEY
(*Grinning*)

That's okay, Mister Roberts. Never thought you'd be taking this ride, did you?
(*He exits with the bags.*)

ROBERTS

I'm going to be off this bucket before I even wake up.

DOC

They flying you all the way to the *Livingston?*

ROBERTS

I don't know. The radio dispatch just said I was transferred and travel by air if possible. I imagine it's all the way though.

They're landing planes at Okinawa now and that's where my can is probably running around. (*Laughs a little*) Listen to me, Doc—my can!

PULVER
(*Studying map by* ROBERTS' *bunk*)
Okinawa! Jeez, you be might-y careful, Doug.

ROBERTS
Okay, Frank. This is *too* much to take, Doc. I even got a destroyer! The *Livingston!* That's one of the greatest cans out there.

PULVER
I know a guy on the *Livingston*. He don't think it's so hot.

DOLAN
(*Entering. He has a file folder under his arm*)
Here you are, Mister Roberts. I typed up three copies of the radio dispatch. I've got to keep a copy and here's two for you. You're now officially detached from this here bucket. Let me be the first.

ROBERTS
Thanks, Dolan. (*They shake hands.* ROBERTS *takes papers, and looks at them*) Dolan, how about these orders? I haven't sent in a letter for a month!

DOLAN
(*Carefully*)
You know how the Navy works, Mister Roberts.

ROBERTS
Yeah, I know, but it doesn't seem . . .
146

MISTER ROBERTS

DOLAN

Listen, Mister Roberts, I can tell you exactly what happened. Those guys at the Bureau need men for combat duty awful bad and they started looking through all the old letters and they just come across one of yours.

ROBERTS

Maybe—but still you'd think . . .

DOLAN

Listen, Mister Roberts. We can't stand here beating our gums! You better get cracking! You seen what it said there, "Proceed immediately." And the Old Man says if you ain't off of here in an hour, by God, he's going to throw you off!

ROBERTS

Is that all he said?

DOLAN

That's all he said.

ROBERTS

(*Grinning at* DOC)

After fighting this for two years you'd think he'd say more than that . . .

CAPTAIN'S VOICE

(*Offstage*)

Be careful of that one. Put it down easy.

DOC

What's that?

DOLAN

A new enlarged botanical garden. That's why he can't even be bothered about you today, Mister Roberts. Soon as we anchored this morning he sent Olsen over with a special detail—they dug up two palm trees . . . He's busy as a mother skunk now and you know what he's done—he's already set

147

a twenty-four-hour watch on these new babies with orders to shoot to kill. (*To* PULVER) That reminds me, Mister Pulver. The Captain wants to see you right away.

PULVER

Yeah? What about?

DOLAN

I don't know, sir. (*To* ROBERTS) I'll be back to say good-bye, Mister Roberts. Come on, Mister Pulver. (*He exits.*)

PULVER
(*Following* DOLAN *out*)
What the hell did I do with his laundry this week?
(ROBERTS *smiles as he starts putting on his black tie.*)

DOC

You're a happy son-of-a-bitch, aren't you?

ROBERTS

Yep. You're happy about it too, aren't you, Doc?

DOC

I think it's the only thing for you. (*Casually*) What do you think of the crew now, Doug?

ROBERTS

We're all right now. I think they're nice guys—all of them.

DOC

Unh-hunh. And how do you think they feel about you?

ROBERTS

I think they like me all right . . . till the next guy comes along.

DOC

You don't think you're necessary to them?

ROBERTS

(*Sitting on bunk*)

Hell, no. No officer's necessary to the crew, Doc.

DOC

Are you going to leave this ship believing that?

ROBERTS

That's nothing against them. A crew's too busy looking after themselves to care about anyone else.

DOC

Well, take a good, deep breath, Buster. (*He drinks some alcohol*) What do you think got you your orders? Prayer and fasting? Sending in enough Wheatie box tops?

ROBERTS

My orders? Why, what Dolan said—one of my old letters turned up . . .

DOC

Bat crap! This crew got you transferred. They were so busy looking out for themselves that they took a chance of landing in prison for five years—any one of them. Since you couldn't send in a letter for transfer, they sent one in for you. Since they knew the Captain wouldn't sign it approved, they didn't bother him—they signed it for him.

149

ROBERTS

What do you mean? They forged the Captain's name?

DOC

That's right.

ROBERTS
(*Rising*)
Doc! Who did? Which one of them?

DOC

That would be hard to say. You see, they had a mass meeting down in the compartment. They put guards at every door. They called it the Captain's-Name-Signing contest. And every man in this crew—a hundred and sixty-seven of them—signed the Captain's name on a blank sheet of paper. And then there were judges who compared these signatures with the Captain's and selected the one to go in. At the time there was some criticism of the decision on the grounds that the judges were drunk, but apparently, from the results, they chose well.

ROBERTS

How'd you find out about this, Doc?

DOC

Well, it was a great honor. I am the only officer aboard who does know. I was a contestant. I was also a judge. This double honor was accorded me because of my character, charm, good looks and because the medical department contributed four gallons of grain alcohol to the contest. (*Pauses*) It was quite a thing to see, Doug. A hundred and sixty-seven guys with only one idea in their heads—to do something for Mister Roberts.

150

ROBERTS

(*After a moment*)

I wish you hadn't told me, Doc. It makes me look pretty silly after what I just said. But I didn't mean it, Doc. I was afraid to say what I really feel. I love those bastards, Doc. I think they're the greatest guys on this earth. All of a sudden I feel that there's something wrong—something terribly wrong —about leaving them. God, what can I say to them?

DOC

You won't say anything—you don't even know. When you're safely aboard your new ship I'm supposed to write and tell you about it. And at the bottom of the letter, I'm supposed to say, "Thanks for the liberty, Mister Roberts. Thanks for everything."

ROBERTS

Jesus!

(PULVER *enters, downcast.*)

PULVER

I'm the new Cargo Officer. And that's not all—I got to have dinner with him tonight. He *likes* me!

(*There is a polite rap on the door.*)

DOC

Come in.

(*Enter* PAYNE, REBER, GERHART, SCHLEMMER, DOLAN *and* INSIGNA, *all carrying canteen cups except* INSIGNA *whose cup is in his belt. He carries a large, red fire extinguisher.*)

What's this?

INSIGNA

Fire and rescue party. Heard you had a fire in here.

(*All are looking at* ROBERTS.)

ROBERTS

No, but—since you're here—I—

INSIGNA

Hell, we got a false alarm then. Happens all the time. (*Sets extinguisher on desk*) In that case, we might as well drink this stuff. Give me your glass, Mister Roberts, and I'll put a head on it—yours too, Doc. I got one for you, Mister Pulver. (*He fills their glasses from the fire extinguisher.*)

ROBERTS

What's in that, a new batch of jungle juice?

INSIGNA

Yeah, in the handy, new, portable container. Everybody loaded?
(*All nod.*)

DOLAN

Go ahead, Sam.

INSIGNA
(*To* ROBERTS)

There's a story going around that you're leaving us. That right?

ROBERTS
(*Carefully*)

That's right, Sam. And I . . .

INSIGNA

Well, we didn't want you to get away without having a little drink with us and we thought we ought to give you a little sort of going-away present. The fellows made it down in the machine shop. It ain't much but we hope you like it. (REBER

152

prompts him) We all sincerely hope you like it. (*Calls off-stage*) All right, you bastards, you can come in now.

> (*Enter* LINDSTROM, MANNION, DOWDY *and* STEFANOWSKI. MANNION *is carrying a candy box. He walks over to* ROBERTS *shyly and hands him the box.*)

ROBERTS

What is it?

SCHLEMMER

Open it.

> (ROBERTS *opens the box. There is a deep silence.*)

PULVER

What is it, Doug?

> (ROBERTS *holds up the box. In it is a brass medal shaped like a palm tree attached to a piece of gaudy ribbon.*)

LINDSTROM

It's a palm tree, see.

DOLAN

It was Dowdy's idea.

DOWDY

Mannion here made it. He cut it out of sheet brass down in the machine shop.

INSIGNA

Mannion drilled the words on it too.

MANNION

Stefanowski thought up the words.

STEFANOWSKI
> (*Shoving* LINDSTROM *forward*)

Lindstrom gets credit for the ribbon from a box of candy that his sister-in-law sent him. Read the words, Mister Roberts.

ROBERTS
(*With difficulty*)
"Order . . . order of . . ."
(*He hands the medal to* DOC.)

DOC
(*Rises and reads solemnly*)
"Order of the palm. To Lieutenant (jg) Douglas Roberts for action against the enemy, above and beyond the call of duty on the night of eight May 1945."
(*He passes the medal back to* ROBERTS.)

ROBERTS
(*After a moment—smiling*)
It's very nice but I'm afraid you've got the wrong guy.
(*The men turn to* DOWDY, *grinning.*)

DOWDY
We know that, but we'd kinda like for you to have it anyway.

ROBERTS
All right, I'll keep it.
(*The men beam. There is an awkward pause.*)

GERHART
Stefanowski thought up the words.

ROBERTS
They're fine words.
(WILEY *enters.*)

WILEY
The boat's here, Mister Roberts. I put your gear in. They want to shove off right away.

ROBERTS

(*Rising*)

Thanks. We haven't had our drink yet.

REBER

No, we ain't.

(*All get to their feet.* ROBERTS *picks up his glass, looks at the crew, and everyone drinks.*)

ROBERTS

Good-bye, Doc.

DOC

Good-bye, Doug.

ROBERTS

And thanks, Doc.

DOC

Okay.

ROBERTS

Good-bye, Frank.

PULVER

Good-bye, Doug.

ROBERTS

Remember, I'm counting on you.

PULVER *nods.* ROBERTS *turns to the crew and looks at them for a moment. Then he takes the medal from the box, pins it on his shirt, shows it to them, then gives a little gestured salute and exits as the lights*

Fade Out

During the darkness we hear voices making announcements over the squawk box:

FIRST VOICE

Now hear this . . . now hear this . . . Sweepers, man your brooms. Clean sweep-down fore and aft!

SECOND VOICE

Now hear this! All men put on report today will fall in on the quarter-deck—and form three ranks!

THIRD VOICE

Now hear this! All divisions will draw their mail at 1700—in the mess hall.

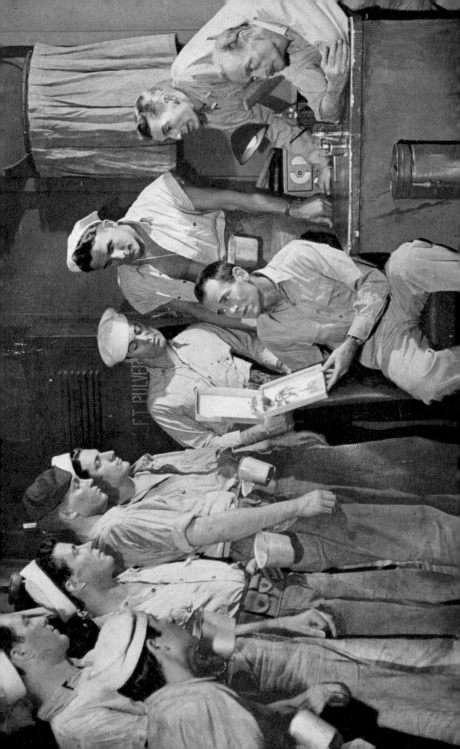

Scene VI

The lights come up showing the main set at sunset. DOC *is sitting on the hatch, reading a letter.* MANNION, *wearing side-arms, is pacing up and down in front of the* CAPTAIN'S *cabin. On each side of the door is a small palm tree in a five-gallon can—on one can is painted in large white letters, "Keep Away"; on the other, "This Means You." After a moment,* PULVER *enters from the left passageway, carrying a small packet of letters.*

PULVER

Hello, Mannion. Got your mail yet?

MANNION

No. I've got the palm tree watch.

PULVER

Oh. (*To* DOC) What's your news, Doc?

DOC

My wife got some new wallpaper for the living room.
(PULVER *sits on hatch cover.* DOWDY *enters wearing work gloves.*)

DOWDY

Mister Pulver, we'll be finished with the cargo in a few minutes.

PULVER

How'd it go?

157

MISTER ROBERTS

DOWDY

Not bad. I've got to admit you were right about Number Three hold. It worked easier out of there. Mister Pulver, I just found out what the Captain decided—he ain't going to show a movie again tonight.

PULVER

Why not?

DOWDY

He's still punishing us because he caught Reber without a shirt on two days ago. You've got to go in and see him.

PULVER

I did. I asked him to show a movie yesterday.

DOWDY

Mister Pulver, what the hell good does that do us today? You've got to keep needlin' that guy—I'm tellin' you.

PULVER

Don't worry. I'll take care of it in my own way.

DOWDY

(*Going off, but speaking loud enough to be heard*)
Oh, God, no movie again tonight.
(*He exits.* PULVER *starts looking at his packet of mail.*)

PULVER

(*Looking at first letter*)
This is from my mother. All she ever says is stay away from Japan. (*He drops it on the hatch cover*) This is from Alabama. (*Puts it in his pocket and pats it. Looks at third letter*) Doc! This is from Doug!

158

DOC

Yeah? (PULVER *rips open the envelope*) What does he say?

PULVER

(*Reading*)

"This will be short and sweet, as we're shoving off in about two minutes . . ." (*Pauses and remarks*) This is dated three weeks ago.

DOC

Does he say where he is?

PULVER

Yeah. He says: "My guess about the location of this ship was just exactly right." (*Looks up*) That means he's around Okinawa all right! (*Reads on and chuckles*) He's met Fornell. That's that friend of mine . . . a guy named Fornell I went to college with. Listen to this: "Fornell says that you and he used to load up your car with liquor in Omaha and then sell it at an indecent profit to the fraternity boys at Iowa City. How about that?" We did too. (*Smiles happily*) "This part is for Doc." (DOC *gestures for him to read it*) "I've been aboard this destroyer for two weeks now and we've already been through four air attacks. I'm in the war at last, Doc. I've caught up with that task force that passed me by. I'm glad to be here. I had to be here, I guess. But I'm thinking now of you, Doc, and you, Frank, and Dolan and Dowdy and Insigna and everyone else on that bucket—all the guys everywhere who sail from Tedium to Apathy and back again—with an occasional side trip to Monotony. This is a tough crew on here, and they have a wonderful battle record. But I've discovered, Doc, that the most terrible enemy of this war is the boredom that eventually becomes a faith and, therefore, a sort of suicide—and I know now that the ones who refuse to surrender to it are the strongest of all.

"Right now, I'm looking at something that's hanging over my desk: a preposterous hunk of brass attached to the most bilious piece of ribbon I've ever seen. I'd rather have it than the Congressional Medal of Honor. It tells me what I'll always be proudest of—that at a time in the world when courage counted most, I lived among a hundred and sixty-seven brave men.

"So, Doc, and especially you, Frank, don't let those guys down. Of course, I know that by this time they must be very happy because the Captain's overhead is filled with marbles and . . ." (*He avoids* DOC's *eyes*) "Oh, hell, here comes the mail orderly. This has to go now. I'll finish it later. Meanwhile you bastards can write too, can't you?

"Doug."

DOC

Can I see that, Frank?

(PULVER *hands him the letter, looks at the front of his next letter and says quietly:*)

PULVER

Well, for God's sake, this is from Fornell!

DOC

(*Reading* ROBERTS' *letter to himself*)

". . . I'd rather have it than the Congressional Medal of Honor." I'm glad he found that out. (*He looks at* PULVER, *sensing something wrong*) What's the matter? (PULVER *does not answer*) What's the matter, Frank?

(PULVER *looks at him slowly as* DOWDY *enters.*)

MISTER ROBERTS

DOWDY

All done, Mister Pulver. We've secured the hatch cover.
No word on the movie, I suppose.

DOC

(Louder, with terror)

Frank, what is it?

PULVER

Mister Roberts is dead. *(Looks at letter)* This is from Fornell . . . They took a Jap suicide plane. It killed everyone in
a twin-forty battery and then it went on through and killed
Doug and another officer in the wardroom. *(Pause)* They
were drinking coffee when it hit.

DOWDY

(Quietly)

Mister Pulver, can I please give that letter to the crew?

DOC

No. *(Holding out* ROBERTS' *letter)* Give them this one. It's
theirs. (DOWDY *removes gloves and takes the letter from* DOC
and goes off) Coffee . . .

    (PULVER *gets up restlessly.* DOC *stares straight ahead.*
    PULVER *straightens. He seems to grow. He walks cas-
    ually over to* MANNION.)

PULVER

(In a friendly voice)

Go on down and get your mail. I'll stand by for you.

MANNION

(Surprised)

You will? Okay, thanks, Mister Pulver.

(MANNION *disappears down hatch. As soon as he exits* PULVER *very calmly jerks the rooted palms, one by one, from their containers and throws them over the side.* DOC *looks up to see* PULVER *pull second tree.* DOC *ducks as tree goes past him. Then* PULVER *knocks loudly on the* CAPTAIN'S *door.*)

CAPTAIN
(*Offstage. His voice is very truculent*)
Yeah. Who is it?

PULVER
Captain, this is Ensign Pulver. I just threw your palm trees overboard. Now what's all this crap about no movie tonight?
He throws the door open, banging it against the bulkhead, and is entering the CAPTAIN'S *cabin as*

The Curtain Falls

MLib